Land Mammals
of Southern Africa
A field guide

D1434236

Land Mammals
of Southern Africa
A field guide
Revised Edition

Reay HN Smithers
Illustrations by Clare Abbott

ISBN 1868 12 401 0

Second edition, first impression 1992
Second edition, second impression 1994

Published by
Southern Book Publishers (Pty) Ltd
PO Box 3103, Halfway House 1685

Previously published by
Macmillan South Africa (Publishers) (Pty) Ltd

Cover design by Clare Abbott
Illustrations by Clare Abbott
Set in 9 on 11 pt Megaron by
Unifoto, Cape Town
Printed and bound by National Book Printers, Goodwood, Cape

FOREWORD

Of all the riches with which southern Africa is blessed its mammal fauna is among the most striking, both in its diversity and beauty. It is a fauna running to 291 land-mammal species, including 73 different bats, 78 rodents, 37 carnivores and 44 ungulates. Public interest in these remarkable animals has developed greatly in recent years and so has the need for a concise guide to the mammals, suitable for use in the field. It would not have been possible to find a more suitable author of such a guide than Dr Reay Smithers who, for 30 years, served with great distinction as Director of the National Museums of Zimbabwe. During this time he spent many months in the field, frequently accompanied by his wife Hazel, herself a wildlife enthusiast, documenting the mammal fauna of Zimbabwe, Botswana, Mozambique and other adjacent areas. In this pioneering enterprise he continued in the tradition of Austin Roberts, building up a superb and meticulously curated research collection of mammals, now housed in the National Museum of Bulawayo. Those field investigations led to many significant publications, including a handbook on *The Mammals of Rhodesia, Zambia and Malawi*, published in 1966 and illustrated by the well-known American artist E. J. Bierly, and *The Mammals of Botswana*, which appeared in 1971.

People with the vitality and enthusiasm of Reay Smithers may retire from their official positions but not from their interest in natural history. In fact it is not unusual for natural historians to make their greatest contibutions late in their careers, when the benefits of a lifetime devoted to study and observation come to their natural fruition. So after Reay Smithers had stepped down from his museum directorship in 1976 he accepted an invitation from Professor John Skinner to write a major book on southern African mammals at the Mammal Research Institute in Pretoria. The result, *The Mammals of the Southern African Subregion*, appeared in 1983 and is a unique work of unparalleled comprehensiveness, richly illustrated by Clare Abbott – an indispensable source of information for anyone interested in African mammals. But, as one might expect, this is not a book to be carried into the field – it runs to 736 pages and weighs 3,3 kg!

Hence the need for the present field guide to the land mammals of southern Africa, in the production of which Reay Smithers has once again teamed up with artist Clare Abbott and also with the publishing expertise and enterprise of Macmillan. The result is a concise handbook where 197 mammal species are described and illustrated in colour – an invaluable work of ready reference which surely will be used and appreciated by wildlife enthusiasts for many years to come.

C.K. BRAIN
Director
Transvaal Museum

ACKNOWLEDGEMENTS

This field guide is based on the information that was gathered together for the purposes of producing a reference book on the mammals of southern Africa (Smithers, 1983). It would therefore be proper to acknowledge the work of all those persons mentioned in the acknowledgements to this larger work, which indeed would mean a repetition of that part of the publication. As the principal aim is to keep this guide to a transportable size, this is not possible and I hope that all those mentioned previously will again accept my grateful thanks for their part in the larger work which makes this present one possible.

Again, the names of some 1 300 workers appeared as first authors of papers or books in the bibliography of Smithers (1983) and many of their names, either alone or with co-authors, appeared on several occasions in that bibliography. It is just not possible to list all the publications on which the information presented is based and the bibliography in this guide therefore lists only the most important publications dealing with the mammals that occur in southern Africa.

I extend my thanks to Dr I.L. Rautenbach, Curator of Mammals at the Transvaal Museum, for reading and correcting the manuscript and to Mrs Wendy Simpson for a similar service. The coloured illustrations and drawings that do so much to enhance the usefulness of this field guide were prepared by Mrs Clare Abbott of Johannesburg and speak for themselves. The spoor drawings were prepared from sketches, casts and photographs made in the field by my wife, Mrs Hazel Smithers, who also commented on the text and encouraged me in the undertaking. I should like also to express thanks to Miss Ingrid Vis of the University of Pretoria for her quick and accurate typing of the manuscript. Although the major part of the writing was complete prior to my joining the staff of the Transvaal Museum, the completion of the project took place after I joined, and I have to thank the Director, Dr C.K. Brain, for his permission to complete the work as part of my responsibilities to the organisation. Both for purposes of checking the text and for use by the artist it was necessary to borrow material from the collections of the Transvaal Museum and I have to thank the Curator of Mammals, Dr I.L. Rautenbach, for this facility.

Through the good offices of at first Miss Eleanor-Mary Cadell and later Mr Basil van Rooyen of Macmillan South Africa, close relations were maintained between all parties concerned in the project, which did much to ensure the most harmonious co-operation towards its completion.

PREFACE

Zoology, like any science, progresses by continually assimilating new results into its body of knowledge. So it is that any book on zoology sooner or later needs updating if it is to reflect the current state of the science. The first edition of Reay Smithers' *Land Mammals of Southern Africa, a Field Guide* was completed in 1985 and published in 1986, and was based largely on information collected for the monumental *The Mammals of the Southern African Subregion,* which was published in 1983 and contained information from the scientific literature published up to 1982. During the subsequent decade sufficient new work on southern Africa's mammals was completed, despite increasingly bleak funding levels, for an update of this field guide to be necessary and worthwhile.

Sadly Reay Smithers died in 1987 when his revision of *The Mammals of the Southern African Subregion* was three-quarters complete; had he been spared to finish it, the revised version could have been used as a basis for this updating of his field guide. As it is, to ensure that this updated edition contained the most accurate and most recent information local specialists were invited to submit their suggestions as to where the text of the 1986 edition could be amended or supplemented to incorporate new findings.

The willingness and thoroughness with which the contributors undertook their task are a measure of the high regard in which Reay Smithers and his work are held by southern Africa's zoologists.

The contributors to this updated edition were:

Insectivores and Elephant Shrews: Nico Dippenaar, Transvaal Museum.
Golden Moles: Gary Bronner, Department of Mammals, Transvaal Museum.
Bats and Rodents: Naas Rautenbach, Transvaal Museum.
Rabbits and Hares: Andrew Duthie, Wildlife Society.
Large Carnivores: Gus Mills, National Parks Board.
Aardwolf: Philip Richardson, Mammal Research Institute, University of Pretoria.
Canids: Andrew McKenzie, Mammal Research Institute, University of Pretoria.
Mustelids: Dave Rowe-Rowe, Natal Parks Board.
Viverrids: Brigitte Wenhold, Faculty of Veterinary Science, University of Pretoria.
Aardvark: Christopher Willis, Biological Sciences Department, University of Venda.
Antelope and Buffalo: Michael Knight, National Parks Board.

Mrs Clare Abbott's fine illustrations have been retained.

I should like to thank all the contributors. I hope that they will accept my assurance that it was not through any lack of appreciation of their efforts that not all of their suggested amendments were incorporated. Mrs Hazel Smithers' support for the updating of her husband's work was a source of encouragement for which I am most grateful. The production team at Southern Book Publishers efficiently tackled the complex job of reorganising the altered sections.

PETER APPS
Pretoria

CONTENTS

INTRODUCTION

The aim of this field guide is to assist anyone interested in the mammalian fauna of the southern part of Africa to identify the species that occur, and at the same time to provide a synopsis of facts about their life histories that may make their observation the more interesting.

The area covered is the mainland sector of the African continent lying to the south of the Cunene – Zambezi rivers, usually known as the Southern African Subregion or, for brevity in the text, simply as the Subregion. Although the Prince Edward Islands, which lie in the Subantarctic zone to the south of the continent, are part of the Subregion, no mention of them is made in the text, as they are accessible only officially and no indigenous terrestrial mammals occur on them, only two introduced species, the house cat *(Felis catus)* and the house mouse *(Mus domesticus),* both of which have become feral on Marion Island.

The Subregion has a rich heritage of wildlife, including 291 species of terrestrial or land-living mammals. Very few people, even among those who have spent their lives in the area, can claim to have seen all of them, for some are found only in remote or inaccessible areas and others lead nocturnal or subterranean lives. Most of them are secretive and tend to avoid contact with man, but there are nevertheless some 197 species which, either by chance or design, may be seen, and it is these that are illustrated or given prominence in the text. The remainder are listed next to the description of their nearest relative, with a note on where they occur and other points of general interest.

Field guides have to be portable; consequently the information that can be given can only be a precis of what is known. The reader who wishes to have fuller information should consult *The Mammals of the Southern African Subregion* by R.H.N. Smithers (see "Useful References"). The number prefixed by "S" (e.g. **S24**) at the end of the description of each species is a cross-reference to the species number in the above book.

While the early history of southern Africa, in so far as the handling of its wildlife is concerned, is a sorry tale of thoughtless overexploitation and lack of appreciation of the effects of man's developments, especially on the larger "game" species, the situation is greatly improved today. Sadly, this improvement came too late to save the quagga and the blue antelope (in the latter case, the processes that led to its extinction were in operation long before the first Europeans set foot in the Cape, and probably included competition with sheep, which were introduced about AD 400). Today, species considered to be endangered are the riverine rabbit, the wild dog and the roan antelope, and these are already receiving attention from conservation organisations and research workers.

The growth in influence of organisations and individuals interested in the future of mammalian species, and the introduction of legislation to give power to this interest, are potent factors in the conservation of species. In addition, landowners in the Republic are today appreciative of the value of wildlife as an aesthetic or economic asset, with the result that they have been keen to avail themselves of the opportunities afforded to reintroduce species to their lands from which they had long ago disappeared.

In order to apply conservation measures with wisdom we need to know about the ecology of the species concerned, which can only be achieved with research. The growing number of publications being produced annually shows that there is a healthy appreciation of the necessity of a fuller understanding of this factor. In spite of this, there remains the popular misconception that we know all there is to be known about our mammals. In fact, very large parts of the Subregion have yet to be zoologically explored and we still have to extrapolate on what species live there. We lack a knowledge of the habitat requirements, the habits and many other aspects of the life histories of many of our mammals and the relationship of others remains obscure.

In some cases, particularly the bats and murids, the application of modern techniques to more adequate series of specimens has shown that what we

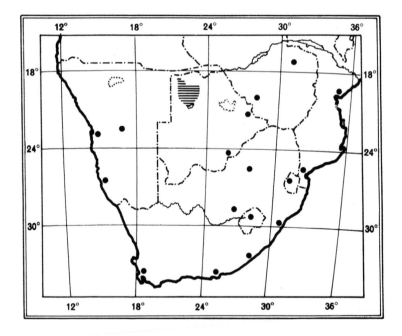

The Southern African Subregion
The northern boundary of the Subregion lies along the northern boundaries of Namibia, the Caprivi Strip and Zimbabwe, thereafter southeastwards along the southern bank of the Zambezi River in Mozambique to the sea.

imagined to be a single population, in which all individuals superficially look alike, is indeed made up of two or possibly more species, which may not interbreed. Much remains to be learnt, especially about our smaller mammals, which constitute by far the larger proportion of species, and until they are studied in detail the information on our mammalian fauna must remain unbalanced, with a great deal known about some species and very little about others.

USING THIS BOOK

Format of the text
For the convenience of readers who may not be conversant with scientific names, the description of each species is headed by its colloquial name, first in English, then in Afrikaans. Recognising that colloquial names may vary regionally, the name chosen is the one felt to be generally acceptable and is that given in Smithers (1983), where, when appropriate, reasons are given for the choice.

The colloquial name is followed by the scientific name, which is that used in the taxonomic revision of our southern African mammals by Professor J.A.J. Meester (see "Useful References"). The scientific names in some cases depart from those used in Smithers (1983). Name changes may cause the layman to think that biologists cannot make up their minds on issues of this sort. This is indeed far from the case, for such changes are a manifestation of an increasing understanding of the relationships of our mammals and arise from the continuing and painstaking study of their evolutionary history and of features such as their skull characters, dentition and genetical composition. As an example, the relationship of Lichtenstein's hartebeest was for a long time a matter of debate. It has now been shown, from the morphology of its skull, that it has a closer relationship to the wildebeest than to the hartebeest, which warrants a change of genus from *Alcelaphus* to *Sigmoceros,* a name that was proposed for it nearly 70 years ago.

Following the scientific name, an indication of the size and mass of the species being dealt with is given, broken down by sex where there are sexual differences. Where adequate numbers of specimens are available this is given in the form of a mean size or mass. While mammal measurements are, by international agreement, given in millimetres (mm), in this field guide they are given in centimetres (cm), as it is felt that the reader can more easily visualise size in this larger unit. When dealing with large species, metres (m), are used and in the case of the antelopes and other very large species the height at the shoulder is given as a measure of size rather than the total length used for the small species.

Measurements used in the text
1. Total length is measured from the tip of the snout to the end of the vertebrae of the tail (A – B).

2. The length of the tail is measured from its junction with the body to the end of the vertebrae (C – D).

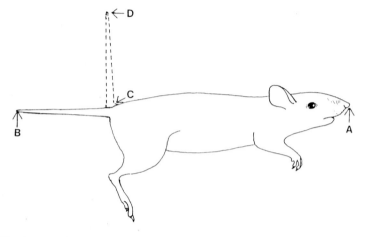

3. The length of the ear is measured from the notch to the tip (E – F).

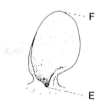

4. The length of the forearm (G – H) is an important measurement in bats.

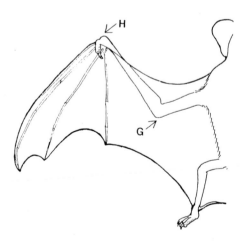

5. Wingspan is the total length, tip to tip, of the fully outstretched wings of a bat.

6. Shoulder height is measured from the base of the hoof or pad to the top of the shoulder.

Distribution

The distribution maps are drawn up on the basis of material records and show the limits within which a species has been recorded, but it should be recognised that, within the limits shown, the species will occur only where there is suitable habitat, notes on which are given in the text.

In drawing up the distribution maps no cognisance is taken of the translocation of species, a process that has been proceeding at an accelerating rate in recent years. The history of translocation remains to be written, but it has played a vital role in ensuring the future survival of species such as the bontebok, the Cape mountain zebra and the square-lipped rhinoceros, among others. For example, the first Game Conservator in Zululand, Vaughan Kirby, estimated that in 1922 there were only about 20 square-lipped rhinoceros in reserves in that sector. This estimate may have been on the low side, but nevertheless, the species was obviously gravely endangered. With careful conservation this nucleus grew in numbers and over the years the Natal Parks Board has made surplus stock available to organisations and individuals both in South Africa and in other African and overseas countries, to the extent that the species is no longer considered to be endangered.

Identification

The emphasis in the text is on the external appearance of the individual species, but aspects of their ecology can often assist in identification. Both in the text and by means of a map, the area in which a species is known to occur is given. This can be of great value when deciding which of various possible species has been seen, and an observation far outside the limits within which a species is known to occur may eliminate it in favour of another known to occur within them.

In the identification of mammals colour has to be used with caution. It is, for example, a common feature of some species of bats that they occur in a number of colour phases. In bats that are most commonly brown or greyish brown in colour colonies are found in which there is a high percentage of golden yellow individuals, or colonies may consist entirely of these brighter coloured bats.

Among species of mammals that have a wide distribution in southern Africa those that occur in the western desert or semi-desert regions tend to be paler in colour than those from the eastern higher rainfall areas. Where there are large numbers of specimens from a wide variety of localities on an east – west transect, in some cases it is possible to see that the gradation in colour is gradual and without any sudden break. Where this is the case the situation is described as an east – west "cline" in colour. Often, in the early days of collecting in southern Africa, specimens were known from only two or three points along this transect, and because of the colour differences, subspecific names were applied to them. It was only when more adequate material became available that it was appreciated that the differences were clinal and the application of subspecific names inappropriate. In species such as the pouched mouse, a common and widespread species, the east – west colour differences are very obvious, and in addition there is a cline in size from north to south.

This situation makes the illustrator's task difficult and all that can be portrayed is a generalised form, while the colour and size differences that occur are noted in the text.

There are, in addition, exceptions to the general colour pattern. In Meller's mongoose, for example, the tail is usually broadly black towards the tip, but individuals with brown tail tips are known and it may even be white, causing confusion with the white-tailed or Selous' mongoose. In turn, in some parts of its range the white-tailed mongoose has a black tail. While the colour of the tail is a very useful character in these nocturnal species, which are usually seen in the beam of a headlight or torch, there are other features, highlighted in the text, that help to distinguish them. Seen at night the two species of genets look very similar, but they can be distinguished as the small-spotted genet has a white-tipped tail, the large-spotted a black-tipped tail.

The habits of a species can also be a useful guide in identification, for some lead solitary lives except at the mating season, while others are gregarious, numbers associating together in herds, troops or colonies. The dwarf mongoose, *Helogale parvula,* lives in troops, and many of the antelope in herds. Apart from its value as a help in identification, understanding the behaviour of a species can enhance the interest and pleasure of its observation. The roaring of a male impala, *Aepyceros melampus,* and the rounding up of a group of females are signs of the onset of the mating season. The curious habit of the male of some antelope species (such as the sable antelope, *Hippotragus niger*), of tapping the hind leg of a female with his front leg, is part of his courtship behaviour and as such is a manifestation of an important aspect of the life history of the species.

What a species eats and where, when and how many young it has at a birth are briefly recorded, as these are questions often put to biologists by persons interested in wildlife.

Difficulties attend the handling of some groups of mammals in a field guide, for in Orders such as the Chiroptera, the bats, and Families such as the

Muridae, the rats and mice, not all of them can be properly identified on external characters alone. No less than 73 species of bats occur in the Subregion and it is likely that other species will be added to the list in due course. The characters that distinguish them lie, in many species, in the configuration of the complicated noseleaf structures and minute processes in the ears (the tragi), which play a part in their powers of echolocation, or in the shape of their skulls and teeth. This means that microscopic examination by an expert may be necessary for correct identification. In these difficult cases the aim of this field guide is to provide information sufficient to assist the observer at least to place them in the appropriate Family.

Fifty-eight species of murids, rats and mice, occur in the Subregion. The question of whether an individual is a rat or a mouse devolves upon size, the dividing line a matter of the observer's own opinion, rats being large, mice small. External characters are better developed in this group than in the bats, and size, colour, proportionate length of tail, fur length and in some species markings are all useful differentiating characters. It is highly unlikely that all 58 species will be seen, as most of them are small and nocturnal, but 33 of the commoner species are dealt with in detail and illustrated and, as in the case of the bats, the remainder are given passing mention, with a note on where they occur.

THE SUBREGION: CLIMATE AND VEGETATION

The Subregion can be geographically divided into a number of zones, which differ from each other climatically and vegetationally and in respect of the species of mammals occurring within them. In terms of geological time the situation is not static but is slowly changing. It has been shown, for example, that the arid conditions in what is known as the South West Arid Zone are slowly encroaching eastwards into the Southern Savanna Grasslands (Acocks, 1975). It is also generally accepted that over millions of years there have been a succession of climatic changes accompanied by vegetational changes that have affected the distribution of mammals.

Viewing climatic change as part of the conditions ruling in sub-Saharan Africa over this long period helps to explain why some species, such as the bat-eared fox and the black-backed jackal, occur today in two discrete populations, one in the drier parts of the Subregion and the other in Somalia and parts of Tanzania. There is good evidence to show that at some time in the past they occurred in the intervening terrain, which today is slightly warmer and wetter and supports a savanna woodland association rather than the open arid association that is a habitat requirement of these species. This swing between the warmer wetter and colder drier climatic conditions continues to operate and has, in the long term, a profound effect on the distribution of mammalian species.

The concern of this field guide is with the present-day situation, but a knowledge of what has happened in the past often explains why some mammals, for example those associated with forest, have a patchy and discontinuous distribution, as in many parts only relic patches remain of what were much more extensive forests in the past. Factors other than changes of climate have, however, also had their effect. The advent of man, especially within historical times, has greatly accelerated the destruction or degradation of habitat for mammals. He has furthermore over-exploited many species to the extent that they have become extinct over vast areas of their former range.

Southern Savanna Woodland

This zone covers a very large part of Africa south of the Congo forests and, with an extension northwards through western Tanzania and Uganda, joins to form a continuum with the Northern Savanna Woodland which extends westwards to Senegal.

In the Subregion it covers most of northern Namibia, northern and eastern Botswana, the whole of Zimbabwe and Mozambique, the northern and eastern Transvaal, and extends narrowly southeastwards along the coast to near Port Elizabeth in the Cape Province. The mean annual rainfall is variable, tending to be higher eastwards than westwards, in the former up to about 900 mm, in the latter 375 mm, but throughout most of the zone about 500 mm. At lower

The main biotic zones of Africa south of the Sahara

ZONES
A Sahelian
B Sudan
C Somali Arid
D Ethiopian Highlands
E Northern Savanna Woodland

F Southern Savanna Woodland
FI Southern Savanna Grassland
G Forest
H South West Arid
I Namib Desert
J Cape Macchia or *fynbos*

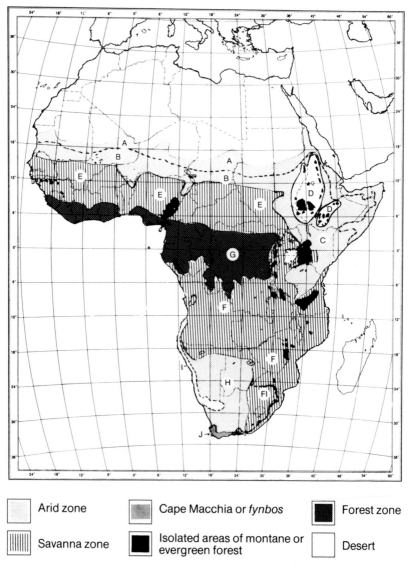

Arid zone

Savanna zone

Cape Macchia or *fynbos*

Isolated areas of montane or
evergreen forest

Forest zone

Desert

altitudes it has a cover of open mopane woodland, in the warmer areas with baobabs, a sparse grass cover and little underbrush. At higher altitudes the drier western areas carry an open woodland or scrub thornbush association, and further eastwards, in the higher rainfall areas, there are well-developed woodland associations of various types with a good grass cover, in parts forming a mosaic with open grasslands or vleis.

This zone supports a rich fauna of browsing and grazing mammals, including many species of antelope.

Southern Savanna Grassland
Bush and tree growth in this zone is largely confined to riverine areas, kloofs and rocky ridges. Mixed grassland predominates, the dominant species being *rooigras,* a highly nutritious grass, which has in many parts, owing to burning and overutilisation, been replaced by inferior and hardier species. The mean annual rainfall in this zone is about 500 mm.

Approximately 30 per cent of the surface area of the Subregion is occupied by this association, which supports the major portion of the maize, dairy, beef and timber industry of southern Africa as well as containing a very large proportion of its human population. In addition to the heavy weight of the developments carried by this association, it has long been recognised (Acocks, 1975) that the eastwards extension of the Karroo associations during the past decades has converted some 52 000 km² of this grassland into an eroded Karroo association (Mentis & Huntley, 1982). This continuing process Acocks viewed as a national disaster.

South West Arid
This zone has a relatively low mean annual rainfall, which varies from about 200 mm to 500 mm in the northern parts to under 250 mm in the southern. The northern parts have an open cover of thornbush or low scrub, with scattered patches of camelthorn trees and a good grass cover on a substrate of Kalahari sand. The southern parts consist of Karroo scrub or succulent Karroo vegetation. Species such as the gemsbok and springbok are particularly associated with this zone, although both utilise at least parts of the Southern Savanna Grasslands eastwards and the desert areas to the west.

Cape Macchia or *fynbos*
This zone has a cool Mediterranean type of climate with relatively humid winters and hot, dry summers. It is often referred to as a winter rainfall area, but winter rains are experienced only in the extreme southwest, west of Cape Agulhas. Rainfall is related to topography and is in excess of a mean of 200 mm per annum, rising in parts of the mountainous areas to over 3 000 mm. The zone has a particularly rich flora of over 6 000 species of plants, but the association generally is fragmented by development and only about 40 per

cent of the original association is left. The mammalian fauna is depauperate but includes a number of endemic species, such as Verreaux's mouse.

Namib Desert

This zone lies as a narrow coastal strip from the Cunene River, the border of Namibia and Angola, southwards to the Orange River and eastwards on either side of the river to the Upington district in the northern Cape Province. The mean annual rainfall is less than 125 mm, much less in the western coastal areas, and the sparse vegetation is supported by advective fogs caused by the cold Benguela current, which sweeps northwards along the coast. Two species of hairy-footed gerbils, the dune and Setzer's, are endemic to this zone, their hairy feet being an adaptation to living on fine, loose dune sand.

Forest

This zone is not a continuum but consists of scattered, relatively small areas of forest in the southeastern and eastern parts of the Subregion. It includes the temperate evergreen forests in the Knysna area of the southern Cape Province, which lies in an area of mean annual rainfall of 760 mm to 1 016 mm. Between the eastern Cape Province and eastern Zimbabwe there are scattered patches of montane and evergreen forest, the former at high altitudes, where the temperature is low and the mean annual rainfall in excess of 1 000 mm. Included in this zone are the coastal and dune forests of the southeastern parts of the Subregion, which in parts have been degraded through man's developments. Species particularly associated with forest include the blue duiker and the red squirrel.

FiELD GUiDE

Order **INSECTIVORA**. Represented in the Subregion by three Families: SORICIDAE, shrews; ERINACEIDAE, the hedgehog and CHRYSOCHLORIDAE, golden moles. They are predominantly insect-eaters, with teeth adapted to this diet. The golden moles live subterranean lives; the rest are terrestrial.

Family **SORICIDAE**, shrews. This Family is represented in the Subregion by 16 species. They have long, narrow, pointed snouts, small eyes, small rounded ears, five digits on the feet, and musk glands on their flanks between the fore and hind legs. They have a high metabolic rate and soon die if deprived of food and water. They are insectivorous, but will eat seed and have carnivorous tendencies. They are capable of making short burrows, but are more likely to use existing cover in the form of rocks or fallen logs, under which they excavate and construct their nests of soft vegetable debris.

While some may be readily identified, others are very difficult and require examination of the teeth and skull of cleaned material.

LONG-TAILED FOREST SHREW Plate 1
(Langstertbosskeerbek) No. 7
Myosorex longicaudatus

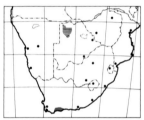

Total length 15 cm, tail about 6,3 cm.

Occurs only in the southern Cape Province, in fern clumps on the fringes of forest and in fynbos on mountain slopes.

The body is dark blackish brown in colour, the underparts slightly lighter than the upper. The species is characterised by its long tail, which is dark above, paler below, and thickened at its base.

Insectivorous, but its diet includes a high proportion of seed. Nothing is known about its reproduction. This species was discovered in South Africa in 1978. **(S1)**

FOREST SHREW Plate 1
(Bosskeerbek) No. 8
Myosorex varius

Total length 12 cm, tail about 4 cm.

Occurs in the southern and eastern Transvaal, northeastern Orange Free State, Natal and Lesotho and in the coastal areas of the Cape Province, in moist, densely vegetated areas.

The upper parts are dark grey-brown, grizzled with fawn or yellow; the hair

1

on the underparts is grey with whitish tips. The feet are off-white, the tail is dark brown on top and paler below.

Nocturnal; it burrows under rocks and uses rodent burrows, lining its nest with soft debris. Litters of up to four are born in spring and summer. **(S3)**

GREATER DWARF SHREW
(Groter dwergskeerbek)
Suncus lixus

Plate 1
No. 1

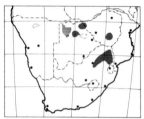

Total length 11 cm, tail 4,5 cm.

Recorded from localities in the northern and northeastern parts of the Subregion.

The upper parts of the body are grey tinged with brown, the underparts slightly paler. The fore and hind feet are white, the tail is brown above and paler below. Little is known about this species. **(S4)**

LEAST DWARF SHREW
(Kleinste dwergskeerbek)
Suncus infinitesimus

Plate 1
No. 2

A tiny shrew; total length 8 cm, tail 2,8 cm.

Recorded from the Cape Province, Natal, Orange Free State and southern Transvaal.

The upper parts of the body are dark brownish grey, the underparts grey. The feet are paler in colour than the body and the tail is dark brownish grey above, paler below.

A forest species, but has been taken in association with termitaria in parts of its range. Insectivorous; nothing is known about its reproduction. **(S6)**

SWAMP MUSK SHREW
(Vleiskeerbek)
Crocidura mariquensis

Plate 1
No. 5

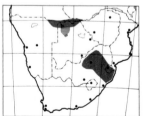

Total length 14 cm, tail 5 cm.

Occurs in the northern and eastern parts of the Subregion in damp places along river banks and on the fringes of swamps; as a consequence its distribution is scattered and discontinuous.

The body is dark brown to blackish brown above, slightly paler below, the tail and feet similarly coloured. The dark colour and moist habitat are a guide to identification.

Active in spells throughout the day and night. Up to five young are born in nests made of vegetable debris on raised patches of dry ground in the wet habitat, usually at the base of clumps of tussock grass. **(S7)**

GREATER MUSK SHREW

Plate 1
No. 4

(Groter skeerbek)
Crocidura flavescens

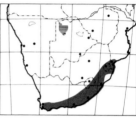

A large species; total length 16 cm, tail 6 cm.

Distribution is discontinuous, owing to its need for a moist habitat with dense vegetation and rainfall in excess of 500 mm per annum.

Variable in colour: in the Cape Province it is reddish brown with brownish grey underparts; in the southern Transvaal it is pale fawn with whitish underparts.

Active in spells throughout the day and night; it is predominantly insectivorous, with carnivorous tendencies. Up to two young are born during the summer, in cup-shaped nests in tussock grass in dry places above the damp substrate. **(S12)**

The closely related **giant musk shrew** occurs in eastern Zimbabwe and northern Botswana. It is larger and is dark reddish brown with pale reddish brown underparts. (See note, **S12**)

LESSER RED MUSK SHREW

Plate 1
No. 6

(Klein rooiskeerbek)
Crocidura hirta

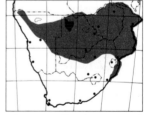

Total length 13 cm, tail 4,6 cm.

Widespread in the northern and northeastern parts of the Subregion, where it is the commonest species found. Catholic in its habitat requirements, it is not uncommon in suburban gardens, nesting in compost heaps. In the veld it tends to prefer damp places.

The upper parts of the body vary in colour: populations in the east are cinnamon brown, with pale silvery grey underparts; in the west they are pale fawn with a faint wash of reddish brown and pale off-white underparts. They have short, thick tails. The feet are usually paler in colour than the upper parts of the body.

Predominantly insectivorous, but has carnivorous tendencies. Up to four young are born in cup-shaped nests during the summer. The females are capable of producing two litters in a season. **(S14)**

3

CLIMBING SHREW

(Klimskeerbek)

Sylvisorex megalura

Plate 1
No. 3

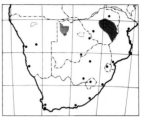

Total length 16 cm, tail 8,4 cm.

At the moment, recorded only from parts of Zimbabwe, where it is found in stands of tall grass and scrub bush.

The upper parts of the body are dark brownish grey, the underparts grey with a wash of white. The characteristic feature is the long tail, over half the total length, which is dark brownish grey above and pale below. The feet are the same colour as the upper parts of the body. Little is known about its life history. **(S15)**

The remaining species of shrew are difficult to identify on external characters. It is recommended that if positive identification is required material should be submitted to a museum.

Family **ERINACEIDAE**, hedgehogs. Although there are six species of hedgehogs in Africa, only one occurs in the Subregion. Hedgehogs are unmistakable, with their pelage of short spines covering the upper parts of their bodies.

SOUTH AFRICAN HEDGEHOG

(Suid-Afrikaanse krimpvarkie)

Atelerix frontalis

Plate 2
No. 5

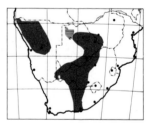

Total length up to about 22 cm.

Occurs in two discrete areas in the Subregion, one in northern Namibia, the other extending in a belt from Zimbabwe south to the Grahamstown district of the Cape Province.

The spines are white at the base, with a broad black or dark brown band in the middle and white or buffy tips; some of the spines are pure white. In some individuals the white spines tend to lie in longitudinal lines from the head to the rump, in others they are scattered throughout the pelage. The face, limbs and tail are covered with dark brown or greyish brown hair, the hair on the underparts either white or totally black or a mixture of the two colours. The

---

Plate 1:   1. Greater dwarf shrew (p. 2).   **2.** Least dwarf shrew (p. 2).   **3.** Climbing shrew (p. 4).   **4.** Greater musk shrew (p. 3).   **5.** Swamp musk shrew (p. 2).   **6.** Lesser red musk shrew (p. 3).   **7.** Long-tailed forest shrew (p. 1).   **8.** Forest shrew (p. 1).

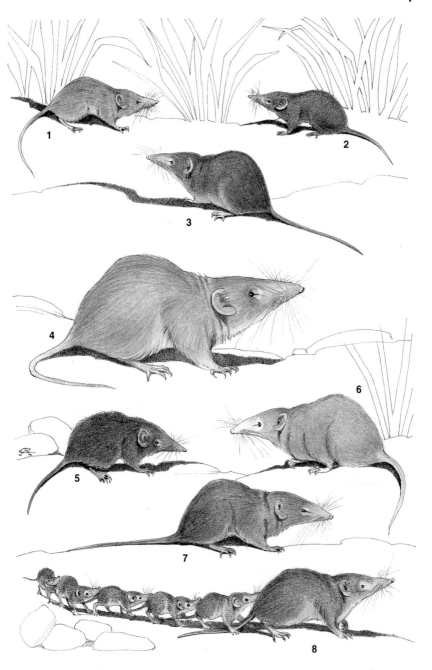

face has a conspicuous white band across the forehead and the snout is sharply pointed. Unlike some other species of hedgehog, it has five toes on the hind feet.

Predominantly nocturnal, often moving about during the day after rain. Hedgehogs rest curled up in a ball in vegetable debris in shady places, spending long periods during the colder months of the year in a state of torpidity, when they are little in evidence. They live predominantly on invertebrates, but will take lizards, small mice, birds' eggs, the chicks of small ground birds and carrion. They are noisy, snuffling and grunting as they forage. Litters of up to nine young are born during the summer.   **(S16)**

Family **CHRYSOCHLORIDAE**, golden moles. Although 15 species occur in the Subregion, golden moles are rarely encountered, as they live subterranean lives. The status of some of the species remains in doubt and others are known only from single localities.

In two species the fur is long and coarse; in the great majority, however, it is soft and woolly, with distinct sheens of various colours. Not all are golden in colour, but in all the forelimbs are short and muscular, with three digits (or in some with a vestigial fourth digit) armed with long claws adapted for burrowing. The hind feet have five digits with small claws and are webbed to help with moving loose soil. They have hard shovel-like snouts to assist in burrowing. Insectivorous, they will take earthworms and some species eat lizards. Most of them are solitary subsurface burrowers, the runs showing on the surface as elevations of the substrate.

GIANT GOLDEN MOLE　　　　　　Plate 2
(Reuse gouemol, kruipmol)　　　　　No. 4
Chrysospalax trevelyani

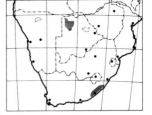

By far the largest species; total length about 23 cm.

Known only from the eastern Cape Province and adjacent parts of the Ciskei and Transkei in indigenous forest and on forest fringes.

Dark brown in colour, the head usually darker, the underparts slightly paler, the fur long and coarse. On the forefeet the first digit is minute with a small claw, the claws on the second and third digits are long, curved and stoutly built.

Plate 2:　**1.** Yellow golden mole (p. 8).　**2.** Cape golden mole (p. 8).　**3.** Hottentot golden mole (p. 9).　**4.** Giant golden mole (p. 6).　**5.** South African hedgehog (p. 4).

2

Unlike the other species the giant golden mole makes only short burrows linked by surface runs. It feeds at night on insects, millipedes and giant earthworms. Nothing is known about its reproduction. **(S17)**

The closely related **rough-haired golden mole (S18)** occurs in the Transkei and in parts of Natal and the Transvaal.

CAPE GOLDEN MOLE   Plate 2
(Kaapse gouemol, kruipmol)   No. 2
Chrysochloris asiatica

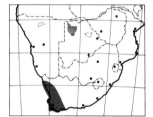

Total length up to 11 cm.
Occurs only in the southwestern parts of the Cape Province in sandy soils or soils loosened by cultivation.
Dark brown in colour, the fur has sheens of green, bronze and purple. The face has whitish eye spots and a buffy line running from these spots downwards to the buffy chin. The underparts are paler and greyer than the upper. On the front feet the first digit is armed with a small claw, the second and third with well-developed curved claws.
The Cape golden mole lives on insects and earthworms and has one or two young during the winter. **(S21)**

The closely related **Visagie's golden mole (S22)** is only known from a single specimen from near Calvinia, Cape Province.

YELLOW GOLDEN MOLE   Plate 2
(Geel gouemol, kruipmol)   No. 1
Calcochloris obtusirostris

Total length 10 cm.
Occurs in the northeastern parts of the Sub-region in sandy soils.
Golden or golden brown in colour, the underparts are paler and sometimes browner or redder. The sides of the face are usually yellower, the snout often with a paler band across the top. The four digits on the front feet are armed with claws, the first digit with a slightly smaller claw than the other two; the third digit is the largest, the vestigial fourth digit carries a small triangular claw.
Insectivorous, and will also take earthworms. No information is available on its reproduction. **(S27)**

HOTTENTOT GOLDEN MOLE   Plate 2
(Hottentot gouemol, kruipmol)   No. 3
Amblysomus hottentotus

Total length up to 13 cm.
Occurs in the southeastern parts of the Subregion and coastally westwards to the vicinity of
Stellenbosch, in sandy soils or sandy loam.
The upper parts of the body are rich dark reddish brown with a bronze,
green or purple sheen; the underparts are pale glossy reddish brown. If
present the tiny eye spots are whitish. The first digit on the front feet is armed
with a small claw, the second with a long curved claw; the claw on the third
digit is the largest and is much broader than the other two.
Lives on insects and earthworms, but will also take snails and vegetable
matter. Up to two young are born early in summer in grass-lined chambers in
the burrows.   **(S30)**

Three closely related species: **Gunning's golden mole (S28)** occurs in a
restricted area of indigenous forest in the northeastern Transvaal; the **Zulu
golden mole (S29)** coastally in the eastern Cape Province and Natal, and
Juliana's golden mole (S31) in the central and northeastern Transvaal.

De Winton's golden mole (S19) and **Van Zyl's golden mole (S20)** are known
only from sandy areas in the northwestern Cape Province; **Grant's golden
mole (S23)** from a narrow strip coastally in the northwestern Cape Province
and southwestern Namibia; **Arend's golden mole (S24)** from eastern Zimbabwe; **Duthie's golden mole (S25)** from the coastal areas of the southern
Cape Province and **Sclater's golden mole (S26)** from the central Karoo,
eastern Orange Free State and southeastern Transvaal. Very little is known
about these species.

Order **MACROSCELIDEA**, elephant shrews. The characteristic feature of
members of this Order is the elongated, trunk-like, exceedingly mobile
snout which carries on its extremity the tiny rhinarium enclosing the
nostrils. They have broad, upstanding, round-tipped ears, which can be
folded back onto the head and, like their snouts, are constantly in motion.
They have large eyes; their hind limbs are much longer than the forelimbs
and they have long slender feet and a naked, glandular patch of skin at
the base of the tail.
They have the habit of drumming the hind feet rapidly on the substrate
when alarmed, which produces a purring noise. The young are born fully
haired with their eyes open and are active from birth.

9

FOUR-TOED ELEPHANT SHREW
(Bosklaasneus)
Petrodromus tetradactylus

Plate 3
No. 3

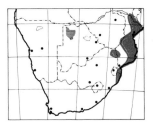

The largest of the Subregion's elephant shrews; total length 35 cm, tail 16 cm.

Occurs in parts of the northeast and eastern sectors of the Subregion in dense underbrush in riparian, coastal and other types of forest.

Colour varies in brightness, depending on place of origin, although the pattern of colour remains constant. The mid-back, from the head to the tail, is reddish brown, the flanks greyish or buffy grey, the underparts white. There are narrow white circles around the eyes, and a dark reddish brown band on the cheeks.

Diurnal, resting in fallen logs, hollow trees or under the roots of trees in pairs or family parties, forming distinct runs from these to feeding sites. The runs are marked by bare patches in the substrate detritus, caused by its hopping gait. When alarmed it vocalises with a shrill squeak. A single young, rarely twins, is born during the summer. **(S32)**

ROUND-EARED ELEPHANT SHREW
(Rondeoor-klaasneus)
Macroscelides proboscideus

Plate 3
No. 5

Total length 24 cm, tail 12 cm.

Occurs in the western and southwestern parts of the Subregion in dry open country with scrub or sparse grass cover.

Very variable in colour, depending on place of origin; those from the southern Cape Province are overall dark buffy grey, those from northern Namibia pale pinkish white, with gradations in colour in the intermediate area between the two extremes. The underparts are white, the grey bases of the hair showing through. It lacks the white eye-rings and pale patches behind the ears that are a feature of other species, and differs from them in the formation of the teeth and in having much larger ear bullae, which show on top of the skull.

Plate 3: **1.** Short-snouted elephant shrew (p. 12). **2.** Bushveld elephant shrew (p. 12). **3.** Four-toed elephant shrew (p. 10). **4.** Rock elephant shrew (p. 13). **5.** Round-eared elephant shrew (p. 10).

1

2

3

4

5

Diurnal and predominantly insectivorous, it lives solitarily or in pairs in burrows, which have entrances under bushes. One or two young are born during the summer. **(S33)**

SHORT-SNOUTED ELEPHANT SHREW

Plate 3
No. 1

(Kortneus-klaasneus)
Elephantulus brachyrhynchus

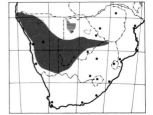

Total length 21 cm, tail 10 cm.

Widespread in the northern and northeastern parts of the Subregion on sandy ground with scrub or grass cover.

The upper parts of the body are variable in colour, depending on place of origin; in the west, reddish yellow, in the east, browner; the flanks are buffy grey, the underparts and upper lip white. Characteristic features are the white circles around the eyes and the rich pale brownish yellow patches behind the ears. The underparts of the feet are brown.

Predominantly diurnal, it occurs in pairs or singly, resting in the cover of fallen logs, piles of debris or holes in the ground. It is a fast mover, and quickly takes to the cover of bushes if disturbed, sitting motionless in the shade where it is difficult to see. It lives on insects, but will take seeds. One or commonly two young are born during the summer. **(S35)**

BUSHVELD ELEPHANT SHREW

Plate 3
No. 2

(Bosveldklaasneus)
Elephantulus intufi

Total length about 23 cm, tail 12 cm.

Widespread in the drier northwestern parts of the Subregion in sandy areas with a sparse grass or scrub cover.

Paler in colour than other elephant shrews, with longer fur; the body is pale yellowish buffy, the flanks paler, the underparts white; those from northern Namibia are distinctly greyer. There are conspicuous patches of pale yellowish brown behind the ears and white rings around the eyes.

Diurnal, living in burrows, which have entrances under bushes. It is insectivorous. One or two young are born during the summer. **(S37)**

ROCK ELEPHANT SHREW

Plate 3

(Klipklaasneus)

No. 4

Elephantulus myurus

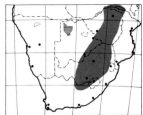

Total length 26 cm, tail 14 cm.

Widespread in the more easterly parts of the Subregion, closely confined to rocky areas.

The upper parts of the body are greyish washed with brown, the flanks buffy grey, the underparts white. The white eye-ring is indistinct. The under surfaces of the hind feet are black and the patches behind the ears are yellowish brown. In overall colour it is greyer than other elephant shrews and its association with rocky areas is a useful clue to its identity.

Diurnal, it lives in crevices in rocks, sitting during the day in shady places from which it sallies forth with lightning speed to secure insects, which are its principal food. One or two young are born during the summer. **(S38)**

Three other species occur: **Peters' short-snouted elephant shrew (S34)** is found only in the extreme northeastern parts of the Subregion; **Smith's rock elephant shrew (S36)** in Namibia and parts of the Cape Province, and the **Cape rock elephant shrew (S39)** in the Cape Province.

Order CHIROPTERA, bats. Seventy-three species of bats are presently known to occur in the Subregion, being surpassed in number of species only by the Order Rodentia, the rodents, with 78 species.

The Order Chiroptera is divided into two Suborders: the MEGACHIROPTERA, fruit-eating bats, and the MICROCHIROPTERA, insect-eating bats. Fruit-eating bats have two claws on the wings, one on the thumb, the other on the first digit or index finger (Pl. 4A); the lower margins of the ears forming a complete circle (Pl. 4C), the tail absent or rudimentary (Pl. 4E), the interfemoral membrane little more than a narrow band along the margin of the legs (Pl. 4E). They lack an ear tragus and have simple cheekteeth without a well-developed cusp pattern (Pl. 4G). The insect-eating bats have a claw only on the thumb or first digit of the wings (Pl. 4B); the lower margins of the ears do not form a complete circle (Pl. 4D), the tail and interfemoral membranes are well developed (Pl. 4F), the ear tragus is present (except in the Rhinolophidae) (Pl. 4D) and cuspidate cheekteeth usually show a well-developed W cusp pattern (Pl. 4H).

Most of the Megachiroptera, the fruit bats, rely on sight to find their way around and locate food. Only fruit bats of the genus *Rousettus* have powers of echolocation as well, and they take advantage of these only in total darkness or when the light level is very low. The emissions are produced as a series of clicks by the tongue, and bounce off objects in their path back to the ears, allowing the bats to orientate themselves in the total darkness of the caves in which they rest. They are classed as fruit-eaters as this is their principal food, but some eat flowers, flower buds or pollen, and others lap nectar. They are represented in the Subregion by seven species, all belonging to the Family Pteropodidae.

The Microchiroptera, the insect-eating bats, are much more diversified and are represented in the Subregion by 66 species divided into 6 Families. They live predominantly on insects, but the large slit-faced bat is known to eat fish and frogs and the common slit-faced bat, scorpions.

While the eyes of the fruit bats are large, and they appear to use sight and possibly smell to locate their food, the eyes of the insect-eating bats are generally small, sometimes minute, and their powers of sight vary, being more acute in some than others. In darkness they have to rely on their powers of echolocation to orientate themselves and catch their insect prey. In simplified terms, this is accomplished by the emission of clicks or bleeps which, bouncing back from objects in the bats' path to their ears, allow perception of the direction and distance of their prey. Their inner ears are the receptors and boosters of the returning signal; their brains the computer that sorts, files and transmits the information to their bodies. In the vesper bats the emissions are uttered through the mouth; in the rhinolophids through the nostrils, the emissions collected and concentrated forwards by the complicated noseleaf structures.

Bats vary widely in their social behaviour. Some, like the Egyptian fruit bat, are gregarious, living in colonies of thousands, others are less so and some are generally solitary. Some are highly specific in the types of shelter they use to hang up in during the day and the method used by the colony in resting. Some hang from the ceiling, others from the walls; some prefer to rest in total darkness, others in half light; some huddle tightly together, others slightly separate from one another. Species such as the yellow house bat prefer to huddle into narrow crevices; others, like Peters' epauletted fruit bat, hang from the branches of trees. The banana bat rests in the rolled up fresh leaves of banana plants, the Damara woolly bat in disused weaver or bishop birds' nests.

Although at the moment 73 species are known to occur in the Subregion, it is quite likely that other species will eventually be shown to be present, and again, further studies may show that what we presently believe to be a single species may in fact be made up of two or more.

A great deal still remains to be learnt about the ecology of this most interesting Order of mammals.

Plate 4:   Bats (Order Chiroptera). Characters of the Suborders.

4

Suborder Megachiroptera: fruit-eating bats.

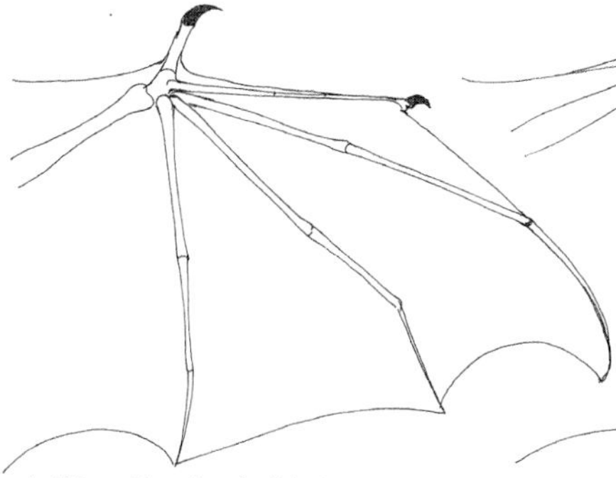

Suborder Microchiroptera: insect-eating bats.

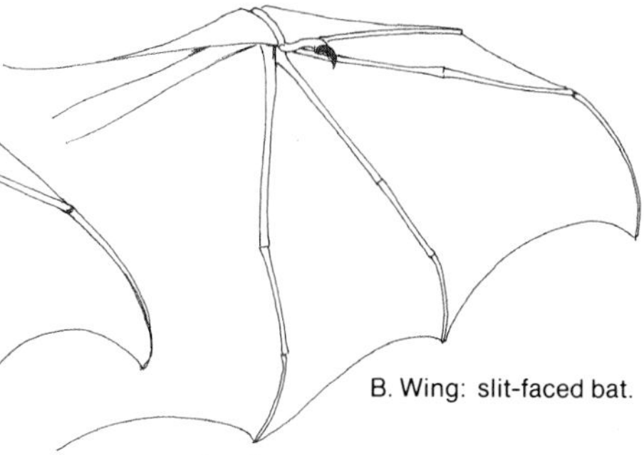

B. Wing: slit-faced bat.

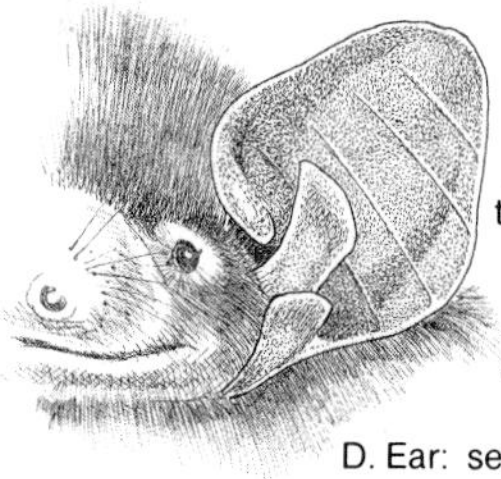

A. Wing: Egyptian fruit bat.

tragus

antitragus

D. Ear: serotine bat.

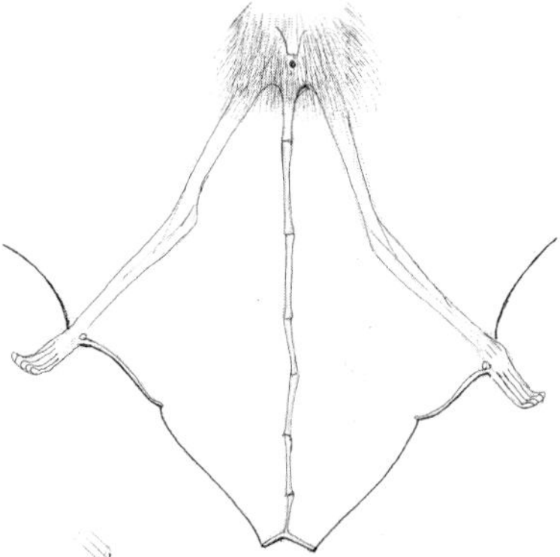

C. Ear: Peters' epauletted fruit bat.

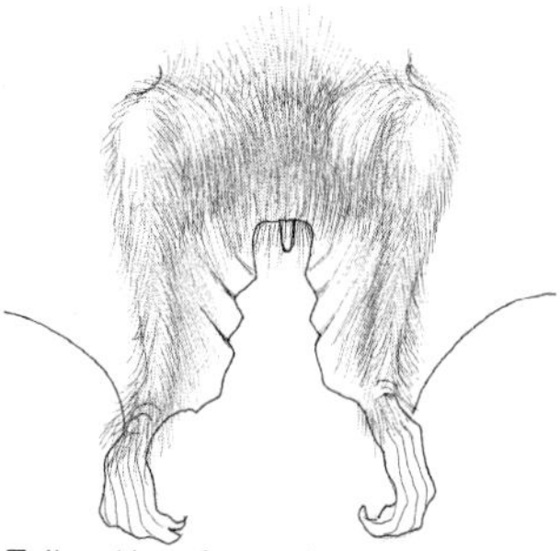

F. Tail and interfemoral membrane: slit-faced bat.

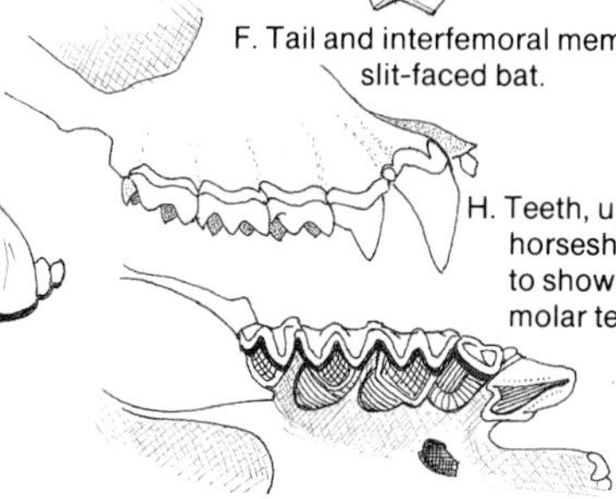

E. Tail and interfemoral membrane: Egyptian fruit bat.

H. Teeth, upper jaw: horseshoe bat, to show cuspidate molar teeth.

G. Teeth, lower jaw: straw-coloured fruit bat.

Family **PTEROPODIDAE**, fruit bats. Seven species of fruit bats occur in the Subregion, all members of this Family. They have simple dog-like faces, devoid of noseleaves, and elongated muzzles (Pl. 5A). The lower margin of the ear is a complete ring and the ear is without a tragus. The tail is very short, often only detectable by touch, and the interfemoral membrane is considerably reduced (Pl. 5D). The most important character separating them from the insect-eating bats is their possession of two claws on the wings: one on the thumb or first digit, the other on the index or second digit (Pl. 4C). They have simple teeth, devoid of a pattern of cusps (Pl. 5F), and large eyes. Their wings are short and broad (the straw-coloured fruit bat is the exception, having pointed wings). The relative position of the ridges on the palate are an important, and in some cases the only effective, means of identifying the species (Pl. 5E).

PETERS' EPAULETTED FRUIT BAT   Plate 5
(Peters se witkolvrugtevlermuis)
Epomophorus crypturus

Total length: males 15 cm, females 12 cm; forearm: males 8,0–8,6 cm, females 7,6–8,2 cm; wingspan: males about 50 cm, females 45 cm.

Occurs in parts of the northern, northeastern and eastern sectors of the Subregion in riverine or evergreen forests or in moist woodlands where there are fruit-bearing trees.

Brown, buffy or nearly white in colour. The underparts are the same colour as the upper, the head tending to be darker than the remainder of the body. Both sexes have white patches at the base of the ears, but only the males have the white patches or epaulettes on the shoulders.

They live in colonies numbering hundreds, resting during the day hanging on the thinner branches of trees with heavy foliage, individuals hanging separate from one another (Pl. 5B). The colonies are very noisy, with much bickering between individuals as they try to settle for the day. The males vocalise with a musical bark. They forage separately in search of wild fruits, using established feeding sites where they hang up to consume the food, the ground underneath littered with unpalatable debris. A single young, rarely twins, is born during the early summer. **(S43)**

Wahlberg's epauletted fruit bat (S40), which is usually darker in colour than Peters', is distinguished from it by having only one palatal ridge behind the last

---

Plate 5:   Fruit bats (pp. 16–19).

16

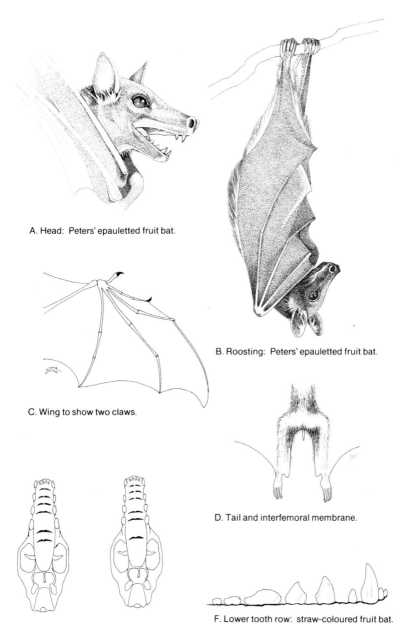

A. Head: Peters' epauletted fruit bat.

B. Roosting: Peters' epauletted fruit bat.

C. Wing to show two claws.

D. Tail and interfemoral membrane.

E. Palatal ridges: (a) Peters' epauletted fruit bat.
(b) Wahlberg's epauletted fruit bat.

F. Lower tooth row: straw-coloured fruit bat.

cheekteeth, Peters' having two (Pl. 5E). It occurs in the northern and eastern parts of the Subregion, often in company with Peters'. The **Angolan epauletted fruit bat (S41)** only occurs marginally in the extreme northwestern parts of Namibia.

STRAW-COLOURED FRUIT BAT Plate 5

(Geel vrugtevlermuis)
Eidolon helvum

The largest bat in the Subregion; the males slightly larger than the females. Total length 19 cm, forearm 12 cm, wingspan up to 70 cm.

Occurs in the Subregion only on migration, the scattered records indicating that it may be found anywhere.

Colour varies from pale yellow to a much darker yellowish brown, the underparts bright yellow. The fur on the upper parts of the body extends onto the forearms and legs and widely onto the wing membranes on either side. The neck has a collar of orange-coloured hair. The membranes and ears are dark brown. The wings are long, narrow and pointed and the apex is capable of being folded for ease of movement when feeding or hanging up to rest. The tail is about 1,5 cm long, the interfemoral membrane very narrow.

Flight is slow, with strong, regular beats, interrupted by gliding, allowing long, sustained, powerful flights, which can carry them over immense distances. This is best demonstrated by the fact that they have been taken resting on ships out to sea, 240 km from the nearest land.

In the Subregion they occur singly, or in small numbers of up to six together, but in East Africa they are gregarious, occurring in huge colonies numbering up to 200 000 (Kampala, Uganda). No breeding is recorded from the Subregion, but in East Africa a single young is born during the summer months, usually in November. The young are carried about clinging to their mothers until they can look after themselves. Their huge wingspan and the fact that they will hang up on power cables renders them liable to electro-cution, many specimens being recovered in this way. **(S45)**

EGYPTIAN FRUIT BAT Plate 5

(Egiptiese vrugtevlermuis)
Rousettus aegyptiacus

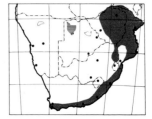

Total length 15 cm; forearm 9 cm; wingspan about 45 cm.

Occurs in the northeastern, eastern and south-ern coastal sectors of the Subregion. Essential habitat requirements are the availability of caves in which to rest and food in the form of wild fruits.

Dark brown in colour; the light-coloured yoke on the neck is a feature of the upper parts of the body. The underparts are pale greyish buff, the throat tinged brown. The wing membranes are dark brown, the fur on the upper parts extending onto the membranes, that on the underparts extending markedly to beyond the forearm.

They live in colonies which may number thousands, resting in caves, hanging from the ceiling or walls, usually by one foot, the other folded across the body outside the enveloping wings. They pack tightly together in clusters deep in the shelter in total darkness. Rousette bats are the only fruit bats with the powers of echolocation, which is used under these dark conditions; otherwise they rely on their keen eyesight. In the northern parts of the Subregion a single young is born during the early summer months; in the southwest, during late winter and early summer.　　**(S46)**

Bocage's fruit bat (S47), a closely allied species, has so far only been recorded from eastern Zimbabwe, and **Dobson's fruit bat (S44)** from northeastern Botswana.

Family **EMBALLONURIDAE**, sheath-tailed and tomb bats. This Family is represented in the Subregion by two genera and three species. The name Emballonuridae is derived from the Greek *emballo,* to throw in, *oura,* a tail, and refers to the tail possessed by all members, one half of which is enclosed by the interfemoral membrane, the outer half projecting from it as if thrown into it (Pl. 6B). This character is unique among bats and renders them easy to identify as members of this small Family. The eyes are larger than in most bats, the ears triangular, with rounded tips and well separated on the head (Pl. 6C). The muzzles lack noseleaves. The shape of the ear tragi is characteristic in the three species (Pl. 6D). The wings are long, the apex capable of being in part folded forwards and upwards, the second part forwards and downwards, thus reducing its length for convenience when resting. The fur is short and soft. When resting they hang with their underparts against the wall of the shelter, scurrying crab-wise to safety when disturbed.

SHEATH-TAILED BAT　　　　　　　Plate 6
(Skedestertvlermuis)
Coleura afra

The smallest of the Family; total length about 7 cm, forearm 5 cm, wingspan about 25 cm.

Recorded only from the northeastern parts of the Subregion, and is considered an uncommon species so far south on the continent.

19

Brown in colour, with pale underparts, the membranes a translucent light brown.

Found in colonies of hundreds, resting in caves in half-light, hanging against the walls, well spaced from one another and separated from other species that may be using the shelter. Nothing is known about their reproduction in the Subregion.   **(S48)**

TOMB BAT   Plate 6
(Witlyfvlermuis)
Taphozous mauritianus

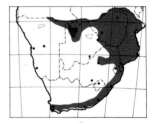

Total length 11 cm, forearm 6,2 cm, wingspan about 34 cm.

Occurs in the northern, northeastern, eastern and narrowly along the coast in the southern parts of the Subregion.

The upper parts of the body are grey, the hairs with whitish tips, giving a grizzled appearance. The underparts are white, the white fur extending onto the transparent white wing and interfemoral membranes. The inside upper parts of the ears are covered with white hair, the outside margins fringed with white hair.

They live in pairs, although two or three pairs may share a convenient resting place which, during the day, may be on the vertical surfaces of tree trunks, rock faces or the external walls of buildings, where there is some overhead shelter from the sun and rain. They hang in the resting places with their underparts flat against the upright surface and if disturbed scuttle crabwise out of sight around corners or into secluded places. Through long-established use their resting places become marked by characteristic brown urine staining. They are sharp and alert and have been observed to take off from the resting places during the day to capture butterflies flying nearby. They hang up temporarily in convenient places, other than the resting places, to consume the food. A single young is born during the summer.   **(S49)**

Plate 6:   Sheath-tailed and tomb bats (pp. 19–22).

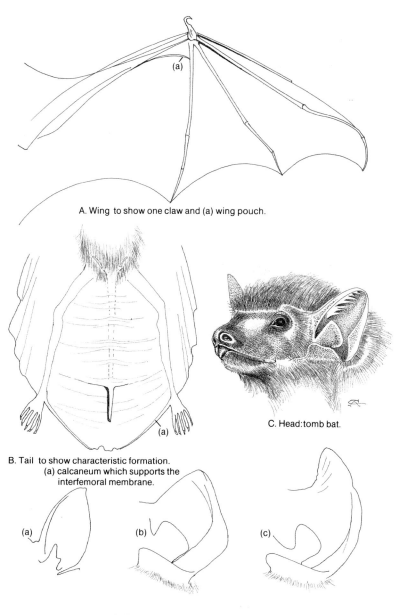

6

A. Wing to show one claw and (a) wing pouch.

B. Tail to show characteristic formation.
(a) calcaneum which supports the
interfemoral membrane.

C. Head: tomb bat.

D. Ear tragus (a) sheath-tailed bat.
(b) tomb bat.
(c) Egyptian tomb bat.

EGYPTIAN TOMB BAT

Plate 6

(Egiptiese witlyfvlermuis)

Taphozous perforatus

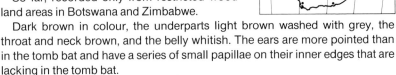

Total length 10 cm, forearm 6,3 cm, wingspan about 34 cm.

So far, recorded only from restricted woodland areas in Botswana and Zimbabwe.

Dark brown in colour, the underparts light brown washed with grey, the throat and neck brown, and the belly whitish. The ears are more pointed than in the tomb bat and have a series of small papillae on their inner edges that are lacking in the tomb bat.

Small colonies of six to eight huddle in the shelter of rock crevices or crevices in stonework, where they remain totally hidden, behaviour markedly different from that of the tomb bat. A single young is born during the summer.

(S50)

Family **MOLOSSIDAE**, free-tailed bats. Fourteen species occur in the Subregion. Members are easily recognised by the characteristic mastiff-like features of their faces (Pl. 7B) and by the configuration of their tails, only the basal one-third to one-half being included in the interfemoral membrane, the remainder projecting free from its hind margin (Pl. 7A). The ears are exceptionally large, roughly as broad as they are high, the pinnae folded back along their inner margin. In some species, the bases of the inner margins of the ears are connected across the top of the head by a broad band of skin. The wings are long, narrow and pointed (Pl. 7A), and can be shortened for convenience when resting by rotating the apices and folding them back upon themselves. The outer toes on the feet, which are heavily built, have fringes of spatulate hair on the sides and long hair towards the tips, the function of which has not been determined. The fur is short and closely adpressed to the body. All members crawl and climb backwards or forwards with equal agility.

FLAT-HEADED FREE-TAILED BAT

Plate 7

(Platkop-losstertvlermuis)

Sauromys petrophilus

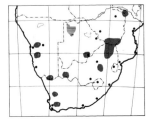

Total length about 11 cm, forearm 4,3 cm, wingspan about 26 cm.

Scattered records suggest a wide distribution in the Subregion, where it is associated with rocky areas.

This bat varies in colour, depending on its place of origin, populations in the

Transvaal being tawny olive, in the west brownish grey and in the south dark seal brown; the underparts are lighter in colour than the upper. The characteristic feature of the species lies in the skull, which is distinctly flattened, allowing the bat to crawl into narrow rock fissures.

They occur in small colonies of up to four individuals, resting during the day in narrow rock crevices, packed tightly together. When disturbed their reaction is to crawl into the narrowest and most secluded parts of the crevices. No information is available on their reproduction in the Subregion.　**(S52)**

MIDAS FREE-TAILED BAT
(Midas se losstertvlermuis)
Tadarida midas

Plate 7

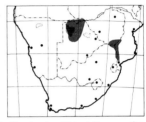

The largest of the free-tailed bats; total length 14 cm, forearm 6 cm, wingspan about 38 cm.

Occurs only in parts of the northern and northeastern sectors of the Subregion, in woodland.

Dark chocolate brown in colour, often sparsely flecked with white; on the upper parts of the neck a band of sparsely haired skin gives the appearance of a light coloured yoke. The throat is dark fawn, the hair on the chest and belly white tipped. The large rounded ears are connected together by a band of skin across the top of the head.

They live in colonies of hundreds, resting during the day in house roofs in total darkness, packed tightly together between the rafters and the roofing sheets. They have also been taken in the interstices between concrete blocks in a bridge. The colonies are very nóisy as individuals jostle and squeak in preserving their position. They are high, fast fliers. A single young is born late in summer.　**(S54)**

LITTLE FREE-TAILED BAT
(Klein losstertvlermuis)
Tadarida pumila

Plate 7

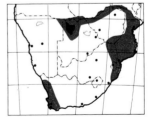

The smallest of the free-tailed bats; total length about 9 cm, forearm 3,7 cm, wingspan 24 cm.

Occurs in the southwestern, northern and eastern parts of the Subregion at low altitudes, usually under 1 000 m.

Colour is very variable, but is more commonly dark brown to blackish brown; some individuals are lighter shades of brown or brown tinged grey. The throat is brown, the remainder of the underparts fawn grey. A pale yoke can be seen on the back of the neck and there may be a crest of long hair between the bases of the ears. Between the upper arm and the thigh there is a band of white hair on the wing membranes.

They may occur in colonies of hundreds but are more usually found in smaller numbers, resting in crevices in brickwork or rocks huddled closely together in their narrow confines. They have also been taken in cracks in trees. They forage singly and are fast, erratic fliers, swooping and twisting in flight. A single young is born during the summer. **(S59)**

EGYPTIAN FREE-TAILED BAT
Plate 7

(Egiptiese losstertvlermuis)
Tadarida aegyptiaca

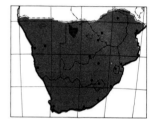

Total length 11 cm, forearm 4,8 cm, wingspan about 30 cm.

Widespread throughout the Subregion, even in the most arid areas.

Dark sooty brown in colour, with similarly coloured underparts, lacking the pale neck yoke of other free-tailed bats. The head tends to be darker than the rest of the body and is often black. The fur of the underparts extends narrowly onto the translucent wing membranes on either side. The ears are not connected at their bases with a band of skin.

They live in small colonies of up to a dozen, resting in caves, rock crevices, hollow trees or behind the loose bark of trees, and have even been taken in crevices in brickwork under the roofs of houses. A single young is born during the summer. Maternity caves with all-female colonies are known. **(S63)**

Of the remaining ten species, three are known from single records; the **Nigerian free-tailed bat (S56),** which has pale wing membranes with conspicuous bands of white hair close to the body, occurs only in northern Botswana and in parts of Zimbabwe, and the **Angola free-tailed bat (S55)** in the northern and eastern parts of the Subregion, the remaining five being rarely encountered and considered as uncommon.

Plate 7: Free-tailed bats (pp. 22–25).

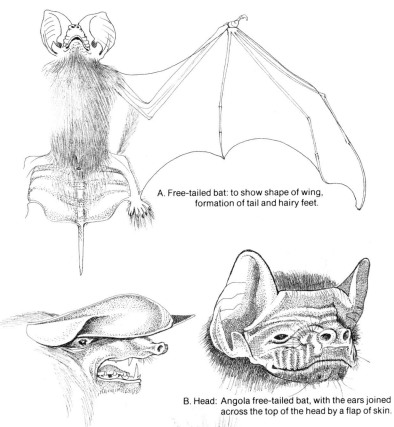

7

A. Free-tailed bat: to show shape of wing,
formation of tail and hairy feet.

B. Head: Angola free-tailed bat, with the ears joined
across the top of the head by a flap of skin.

C. Head: large-eared free-tailed bat.
An uncommon and fast-flying species.
The ear flap closes in flight.

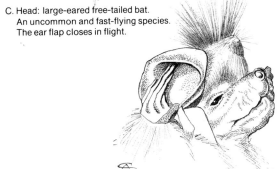

D. Some molossids develop a crest of long hair on top
of the head.

Family **VESPERTILIONIDAE**, vesper bats. This is the largest Family of bats, with 10 genera and 29 species in the subregion. Members are found throughout the world, wherever there is sufficient vegetation to support populations of insects. Characters of members include the simple muzzle, unadorned with nose-leaves (Pl. 8 B & C), the moderately developed, widely separated ears, the long tail, the vertebrae totally enclosed in the interfemoral membrane (Pl. 8A), and the third, fourth and fifth digits of the wing with three joints, a feature shared only with the Molossidae. The ear tragi (Pl. 8B) are well developed and diagnostic of the species. Eight of the more easily recognisable and interesting members of this very large Family are dealt with.

SCHREIBERS' LONG-FINGERED BAT   Plate 8
(Schreibers se grotvlermuis)
Miniopterus schreibersii

Total length about 11 cm, forearm 4,5 cm, wing-span 28 cm.
  Widespread throughout the Subregion, except in the drier western areas.
  The body is deep chocolate brown, the underparts slightly lighter in colour. The wing membranes are nearly black, the wings long and pointed, the tips capable of being folded flat on the under surface, making the wings more manageable when resting or crawling.
  They rest during the day in caves and mine adits, in colonies numbering hundreds of thousands, hanging from the ceilings and walls in tightly packed clusters. Where this type of shelter is not available they will use hollow trees or crevices in rocks. They are migratory, tending to move from cave to cave, and establish maternity caves in which the young are born. They are extremely fast fliers and tend to fly high, swooping in the air like swallows. A single young, rarely twins, is born during the summer. The young cling to their mothers for a few hours after birth and are then left hanging in clusters in secluded parts of the maternity cave while the females forage.   **(S67)**

  Two other closely allied species are recorded: the **greater long-fingered bat (S65)** from eastern Zimbabwe and the **lesser long-fingered bat (S66)**, which occurs in the southeastern and eastern parts of the Subregion.

Plate 8:   Vesper bats (pp. 26–32).

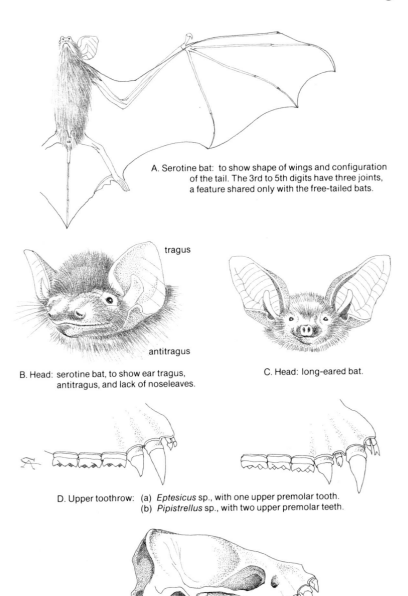

8

A. Serotine bat: to show shape of wings and configuration of the tail. The 3rd to 5th digits have three joints, a feature shared only with the free-tailed bats.

tragus

antitragus

B. Head: serotine bat, to show ear tragus, antitragus, and lack of noseleaves.

C. Head: long-eared bat.

D. Upper toothrow: (a) *Eptesicus* sp., with one upper premolar tooth.
(b) *Pipistrellus* sp., with two upper premolar teeth.

E. Skull: Cape serotine bat.

BANANA BAT
Plate 8

(Piesangvlermuis)
Pipistrellus nanus

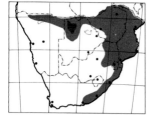

A tiny bat; total length 8 cm, forearm 3,2 cm, wingspan 19 cm.

Occurs only in the eastern and northeastern parts of the Subregion, especially where bananas or plantains are grown or where there are indigenous *Strelitzia* trees.

Varies in colour from reddish to dark brown, the underparts lighter in colour, often with a tinge of grey. The wing membranes are dark brown. The ears are triangular and pointed at the tips and the mouth is large.

They live in small colonies, resting during the day tucked into the thatch of huts or in crevices in roofs, but characteristically clinging inside the freshly sprouting rolled-up terminal leaves of banana plants, up to six or seven head-downwards and closely packed. They also use the curled edges of mature leaves. The thumbs on the wings and the feet are equipped with sucker pads to give a grip on the smooth leaf surfaces. Their flight is unsteady and fluttering. A single young, or twins, is born during the early summer months.

(S75)

CAPE SEROTINE BAT
Plate 8

(Kaapse dakvlermuis)
Eptesicus capensis

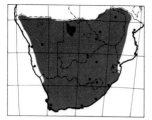

Total length: males 8 cm, females 9 cm; forearm: males 3,2 cm, females 3,4 cm; wingspan about 24 cm.

Widespread throughout the Subregion, except in desert.

The colour is very variable, in darker and lighter shades of greyish brown, the underparts whitish or buffy white, the wing membranes blackish brown. The ears are rounded at the tips.

They live in groups of two or three huddled closely together under the bark of trees, at the base of aloe leaves or tucked away in crevices in the roofs of houses. Their flight is rather slow, sluggish and fluttering, and in foraging they tend to follow a prescribed circular route, jinking and turning in their search for flying insects. A single young, or quite commonly twins, is born during the summer months.

(S86)

YELLOW HOUSE BAT   Plate 8
(Geel dakvlermuis)
Scotophilus dinganii

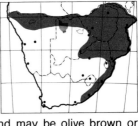

Total length 13 cm, forearm 5,5 cm, wingspan about 30 cm.

Occurs in the northern, northeastern and eastern parts of the Subregion.

The upper parts of the body vary in colour and may be olive brown or greyish olive, sometimes with a distinct sheen; the underparts are usually yellow or have a yellowish tinge, but are sometimes cream coloured with only the faintest tinge of yellow. The ears are small and rounded, the wing membranes brown.

They occur in colonies of up to a dozen, resting tucked into narrow crevices in brickwork under the roofs of houses or between overlapping corrugated-iron roofing sheets. Numbers of colonies may use the same roof, and individuals often enter houses at night when foraging. They also use hollow trees. One or two young are born during the early summer months. For the early part of their lives the young cling to their mothers as they forage.   **(S88)**

TEMMINCK'S HAIRY BAT   Plate 9
(Temminck se langhaarvlermuis)
Myotis tricolor

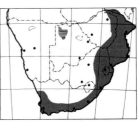

Total length 11 cm, forearm 5,0 cm, wingspan about 28 cm.

Occurs in the southern, eastern and northeastern parts of the Subregion.

The upper parts of the body are coppery red in colour, the paler subterminal portions of the hair showing through, giving the whole a paler appearance; the underparts are whitish, washed with pale coppery red. The wing membranes and ears are reddish brown, the ears long with rounded tips. The fur is soft and woolly and extends onto the base of the interfemoral membrane (Pl. 9A).

They occur in colonies of dozens, resting during the day in caves and mine adits, hanging from the ceilings or walls. They move widely, distances of up to 90 km being recorded. A single young is born during the early summer.   **(S71)**

BUTTERFLY BAT
Plate 9
(Vlindervlermuis)
Chalinolobis variegatus

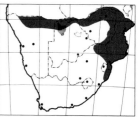

Total length 11 cm, forearm about 4,4 cm, wingspan about 28 cm.

Occurs only in the northern and northeastern parts of the Subregion in woodland.

This is one of the most colourful and easily recognisable species. The body is yellow, tinged with brown; the underparts pale yellow, the wings and interfemoral membranes pale yellow with a bold pattern of dark brown reticulations marking the veins (Pl. 9D). The pale yellowish ears are margined with brown and have rounded tips.

They live in small colonies of up to about ten and rest huddled together during the day in bunches of leaves or in the thatch of huts. They are slow, high fliers, the flight fluttering but then suddenly increasing in speed as they swoop to catch their prey. No information is available on their reproduction in the Subregion. **(S77)**

SCHLIEFFEN'S BAT
Plate 9
(Schlieffen se vlermuis)
Nycticeius schlieffenii

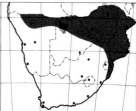

A tiny bat, with a mass of less than 5 g; total length about 7 cm, forearm 3 cm, wingspan about 18 cm.

Occurs in the northern and northeastern parts of the Subregion in woodland, usually at altitudes of less than 1 200 m.

Varies in colour from dark to pale reddish brown, the underparts paler than the upper, the membranes dark brown. The ears are large for the size of the body and have rounded tips.

A solitary species, resting during the day in the roofs of houses, in crevices in the branches of trees or in hollow trees, and congregating to forage. It has an erratic and rather slow flight. Little is known about its reproduction, but females with up to three foetuses have been taken in early summer. **(S90)**

Plate 9: Vesper bats (pp. 26–32).

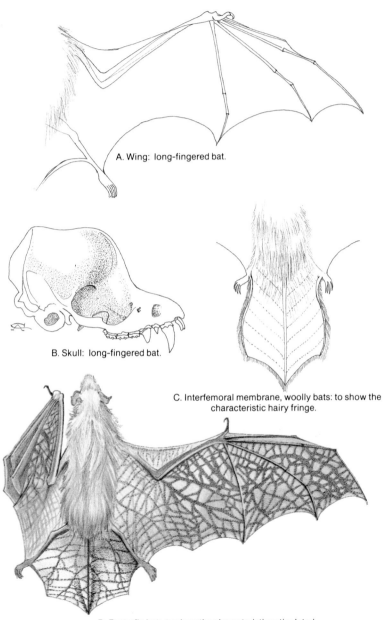

A. Wing: long-fingered bat.

B. Skull: long-fingered bat.

C. Interfemoral membrane, woolly bats: to show the characteristic hairy fringe.

D. Butterfly bat: to show the characteristic reticulated veining on the wing and interfemoral membranes.

DAMARA WOOLLY BAT
Plate 9

(Damara-wolhaarvlermuis)

Kerivoula argentata

Total length 9,3 cm, forearm 3,7 cm, wingspan about 25 cm.

Occurs in the northern and northeastern parts of the Subregion in woodland.

The body is a rich brown colour, many of the woolly hairs on the back with silvery tips, giving it a grizzled appearance. The underparts are greyish brown or whitish, the membranes reddish brown. A characteristic feature of all kerivoulids is the fringe of hairs on the posterior margin of the interfemoral membrane (Pl. 9C). The ears are relatively large and rise to rounded tips.

They are generally solitary, but have been taken in colonies of up to six during the day in clumps of leaves, under the eaves of thatched huts or in disused nests of weaver birds, which appear to be a common resting shelter. They have a slow, fluttering flight, foraging within a few metres of the ground. No information is available on their reproduction in the Subregion.   **(S92)**

The **lesser woolly bat (S93)** is smaller and is found only in the eastern parts of the Subregion.

Of the remaining 18 species of vesper bats, 8 are known from very few records and the remaining 10 require detailed examination of skulls and teeth to be certain of proper identification.

Family **NYCTERIDAE**, slit-faced bats. They are so called as they all have a slit in the skin on the front of the face, which overlies a cavity in the skull housing the paired noseleaves (Pl. 10B), which are visible only when it is opened (Pl. 10C). The ultrasonic emissions used in echolocation arise from the nostrils, the noseleaves no doubt serving some directional or other function.

Members of the Family are easily recognised as they all have long, roughly parallel-sided ears, which in the common slit-faced bat reach a length of 3,7 cm (Pl. 10A). The fur is long, soft and reddish brown or greyish brown in colour; a bright orange phase is also known. The vertebrae of the tail, which has a forked tip, are totally enclosed in the membrane (Pl. 10A). The wings are broad (Pl. 10A) and these bats are expert fliers, avoiding obstacles with agility. After securing their prey, they fly to a feeding site, hanging on a branch or other convenient object while eating, the ground underneath becoming littered with discarded food items. Six species occur in the Subregion, each with characteristically shaped ear tragi.

LARGE SLIT-FACED BAT   Plate 10
(Groot spleetneusvlermuis)
Nycteris grandis

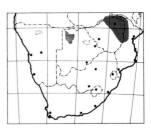

The largest of the Family; total length about 16 cm, ear length about 3,1 cm, wingspan about 35 cm.
Occurs only in the extreme northeastern parts of the Subregion in riverine forest.
Light reddish brown in colour, the underparts paler, with a grey wash.
They live in small colonies, resting in hollow trees or hollow logs lying on the ground, as well as in culverts and holes in rocks. Predominantly insectivorous, they are interesting as they are the only bats in the Subregion known to eat fish and frogs. No information is available on their reproduction in the Subregion. **(S95)**

COMMON SLIT-FACED BAT   Plate 10
(Gewone-spleetneusvlermuis)
Nycteris thebaica

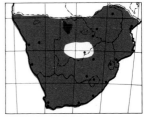

Total length about 10 cm, ear length up to 3,7 cm, wingspan about 24 cm.
Common and widespread throughout the Subregion, with a wide habitat tolerance.
Buffy brown or greyish brown in colour, sometimes in a rufous coloured phase; the underparts are paler, the long ears and wing membranes light brown. Populations in the dry west are paler in colour than those in the east. The fur is long and soft.
They occur in colonies numbering up to hundreds, resting during the day in caves, culverts, mine adits, wells, hollow trees or holes in the ground, often in the roofs of houses or thatched huts in half or total darkness, hanging from the ceiling in scattered groups, not closely packed together like many other species (Pl. 10D). Apart from insects, they will take scorpions and sun spiders, which they pick off the ground. A single young is born during early summer. **(S98)**

HAIRY SLIT-FACED BAT   Plate 10
(Harige spleetneusvlermuis)
Nycteris hispida

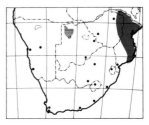

Total length about 9 cm, ear length up to 2,5 cm, wingspan about 28 cm.
Occurs only in the northeastern parts of the Subregion in woodland.

Sepia brown in colour, the underparts paler than the upper and usually greyer. This species and the large slit-faced bat are the only nycterids to have three-lobed upper incisor teeth and they have shorter ears than other nycterids.

In other parts of Africa they rest solitarily or in small colonies in rock fissures, but no information is presently available on this or their reproduction in the Subregion. **(S94)**

GREATER SLIT-FACED BAT
(Groter spleetneusvlermuis)
Nycteris macrotis

Plate 10

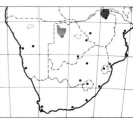

Total length about 12 cm, ear length up to 3 cm.
Occurs marginally in the Subregion, in the Zambezi valley in Zimbabwe.
Colour is warm reddish sepia, the underparts grey. Like the common slit-faced bat, the upper incisor teeth are two-lobed.

In other parts of Africa they rest solitarily in caves, culverts and holes in the ground, and may hang up in bushes or under rocks. **(S97)**

Vinson's slit-faced bat (S99), of uncertain relationship, is known only from the Save River in Mozambique, and **Wood's slit-faced bat (S96)** from southeastern Zimbabwe and the northern and northeastern Transvaal.

Family **RHINOLOPHIDAE,** horseshoe bats. This is an abundant Family, over 90 species of the genus *Rhinolophus* being recognised worldwide, of which ten occur in the Subregion. While individuals can easily be recognised as belonging to the Family, specific identification is difficult, even for workers conversant with bats, as it depends on the configuration of the teeth and noseleaves and other characters apparent only after detailed examination with high-powered lenses. As representatives of the Family, only four of the more easily recognisable species are dealt with.

Plate 10: Slit-faced bats (pp. 32–35).

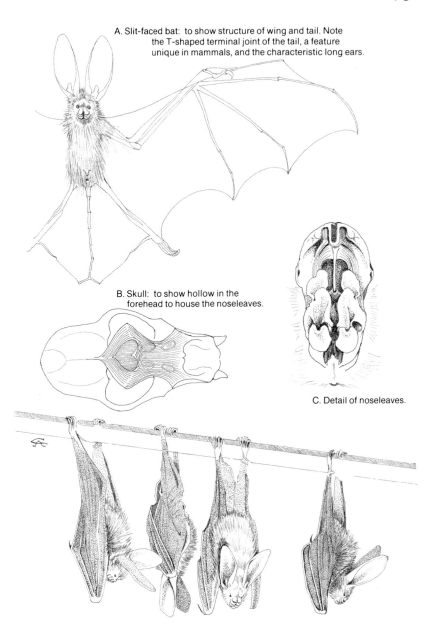

10

A. Slit-faced bat: to show structure of wing and tail. Note the T-shaped terminal joint of the tail, a feature unique in mammals, and the characteristic long ears.

B. Skull: to show hollow in the forehead to house the noseleaves.

C. Detail of noseleaves.

D. Roosting slit-faced bats.

The general pattern of the noseleaves is common to all members of the Family, but varies in detail for each of the ten species. They consist of a horseshoe-shaped process enclosing the nostrils, with a triangular-shaped series of structures arising from it and lying posterior to it between the eyes (Pl. 11B & C). Their function is to channel and focus the impulses emitted through the nostrils, which bounce back from objects in the bat's flight path to the ears and allow flight and capture of prey in total darkness. The ears, which can be moved independently, are large and widely separated; the antitragus or fold of skin at the base of the pinnae is well developed (Pl. 11B(a)) and the ear tragus absent. The wings are short and rounded (Pl. 11A), the flight weak and fluttering.

Even within a species the colour is very variable and reddish or golden yellow phases are not uncommon in populations otherwise more dully coloured. The females have a pair of non-functioning nipples situated near the anus in addition to the functioning pectoral pair (Pl. 12D). There appears to be no size difference between the sexes. The length of the forearm is a useful character in the identification of species.

HILDEBRANDT'S HORSESHOE BAT Plate 11
(Hildebrandt se saalneusvlermuis)
Rhinolophus hildebrandtii

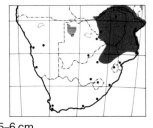

The largest of the Family; total length 12 cm, forearm 6,3–6,7 cm, wingspan 39 cm. Size is useful in identification, as only this species and Rüppell's horseshoe bat have a horseshoe over 9 mm in breadth, the latter with a forearm of only 5–6 cm.

Occurs only in the northeastern parts of the Subregion, in woodland.

Greyish brown in colour, the underparts usually slightly paler. The wing membranes are dark brown. The ears are large, convex on their inner margins, concave on the outer, with pointed tips.

They rest in the cover of caves, mine adits, cavities in rocks or large hollow trees, in colonies that may number hundreds of bats, hanging either from the roofs or walls in total darkness, in clusters of up to 50, the individuals separated from one another. When foraging they frequently enter houses. A single young is born in early summer. **(S100)**

Plate 11: Horseshoe bats (pp. 34–39).

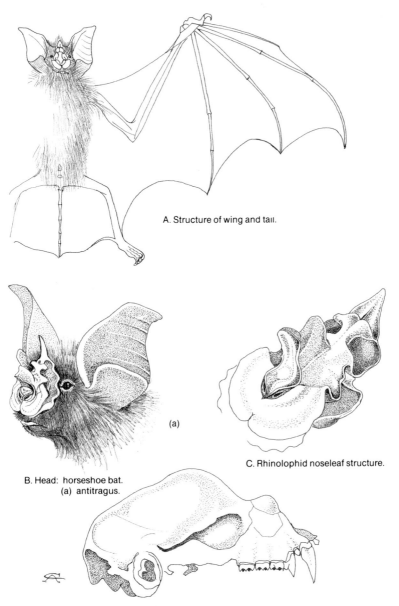

11

A. Structure of wing and tail.

B. Head: horseshoe bat.
(a) antitragus.

(a)

C. Rhinolophid noseleaf structure.

D. Skull: horseshoe bat.

GEOFFROY'S HORSESHOE BAT   Plate 11
(Geoffroy se saalneusvlermuis)
Rhinolophus clivosus

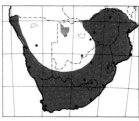

One of the larger species of the Family; total length 9,6 cm, forearm 5,3–5,4 cm, wingspan 32 cm.

Widespread, except in the drier central parts of the Subregion, in a wide variety of habitats from desert to woodland.

The upper parts of the body are light brown, the paler bases of the fur showing through; the underparts are pale buffy grey. The ears are large and pointed, convex on their inner margins, concave on the outer.

They rest in caves, rock crevices and mine adits, hanging from the roofs and walls in clusters, the individuals separated from one another. The colonies number up to 10 000 individuals in caves in the coastal Cape Province. They forage singly, hanging up from branches or under the verandas of houses to consume their prey; these feeding sites are marked by discarded portions of food. A single young is born during the summer.   **(S102)**

CAPE HORSESHOE BAT   Plate 11
(Kaapse saalneusvlermuis)
Rhinolophus capensis

Total length about 8,5 cm, forearm 4,6–5,2 cm, wingspan 30 cm.

Occurs only coastally, in the western and southwestern parts of the Cape Province.

Dark brown in colour, the paler bases of the fur showing through, giving a paler appearance; the underparts are buffy grey. The ears are exceptionally broad and not so sharply pointed as in Hildebrandt's and Geoffroy's horseshoe bats. The wing membranes are dark brown.

They rest in caves, in colonies numbering thousands, hanging from the roofs in clusters, and are often in company with Geoffroy's horseshoe bats, the two species clustering separately. A single young is born during the summer.   **(S106)**

DENT'S HORSESHOE BAT   Plate 11
(Dent se saalneusvlermuis)
Rhinolophus denti

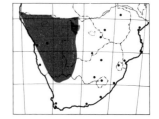

A small species; total length 7 cm, forearm 4,2 cm, wingspan 20 cm.

Occurs throughout the drier central and northwestern parts of the Subregion, wherever there are suitable caves and rock crevices in which to rest during the day.

The colour of the body is imparted to it mostly by the bases of the hair, which may be white or pale cream; the brownish or greyish narrow tips to the hair give the appearance of a wash of this colour on the mid and lower back. The underparts are whitish or pale cream. A golden colour phase occurs. The ears are broad at the base with pointed tips.

They rest in colonies of up to a dozen or sometimes hundreds in semi-darkness in caves and rock crevices. They also use the shelter of the thatched roofs of huts. No information is available on their reproduction. **(S108)**

Family **HIPPOSIDERIDAE**, leaf-nosed and trident bats, closely resemble the horseshoe bats, but differ in the form of the noseleaves, feet and teeth (see Pl. 12). The noseleaves, while possessing the horseshoe-shaped anterior leaflet, lack the posterior triangular processes that are a feature of the horseshoe bats; there is one less premolar tooth on either side in the lower jaw, the total number of teeth being 30 as against 32 in the horseshoe bats, and the toes, except the first, have two joints as against three in the horseshoe bats.

Leaf-nosed bats have large ears, often as broad as they are long, which are set widely separated on the head. The upward fold at the base of the ear, the antitragus, is smaller than in the horseshoe bats, and there is a minute tragus inside the ear. The wings are short and rounded and they have a comparatively slow, fluttering flight. Four species occur in the Subregion.

COMMERSON'S LEAF-NOSED BAT   Plate 12
(Commerson se bladneusvlermuis)
Hipposideros commersoni

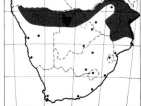

The largest member of the Family; total length: males 15 cm, females 13 cm; forearm: males 10 cm, females 9 cm; wingspan up to 60 cm.

Found only in the northern and northeastern parts of the Subregion and is associated with woodland.

Pale fawn in colour, the head and underparts paler than the rest of the body. The males have a patch of white hair on the sides of the shoulders. The hair is very short and lies closely adpressed to the body. The wings are pale brown, tending to be darker towards the tips; the ears sharply pointed.

They are gregarious and occur in hundreds hanging from the roofs of caves or under the roofs of houses in pitch darkness. Less commonly, they have been taken hanging against the bark of trees and on the outside walls of houses. Nothing is known about their reproduction. **(S110)**

39

SUNDEVALL'S LEAF-NOSED BAT — Plate 12
(Sundevall se bladneusvlermuis)
Hipposideros caffer

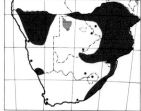

A small species; total length 9 cm; forearm: males 4,8 cm, females 4,7 cm; wingspan about 20 cm.

Occurs in woodland in the northern and eastern parts of the Subregion, with an isolated record from the Orange River mouth.

Colour is no criterion in the identification of this species, as it varies from grey-brown to a bright yellowish golden. The formation of the noseleaves, coupled with size, are the best means of identification, as it is the only small bat found in the subregion with these characters in combination.

They are found singly, in small numbers or in colonies of hundreds; resting in caves, mine adits, culverts, wells or in the roofs of houses, hanging from the ceilings. When in colonies, the individuals hang separated from one another. They are slow fliers, like other members of the Family, but they manoeuvre skilfully, jinking and dodging in flight. A single young is born during the summer. The females have a pair of false nipples situated near the anus in addition to their pair of pectoral nipples.   **(S111)**

SHORT-EARED TRIDENT BAT — Plate 12
(Drietand-bladneusvlermuis)
Cloeotis percivali

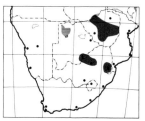

A small species; total length 7 cm; forearm 3,5 cm, wingspan about 15 cm.

So far, recorded only from scattered areas in the northeast of the Subregion.

The colour of the body is slate grey to buffy brown, the head usually tinged yellowish, the underparts grey. The hair is soft and silky and nearly obscures the tiny ears, which are rounded on their outside margins. The characteristic feature of this bat is the three-pronged trident-like processes on top of the noseleaves, which it possesses in common with the next species, the Persian leaf-nosed bat (which is noticeably larger).

They rest in caves and mine adits, in colonies of hundreds, hanging from the roofs in tight clusters, in total darkness. A single young is born during the early summer.   **(S112)**

Plate 12: Leaf-nosed and trident bats (pp. 39–42).

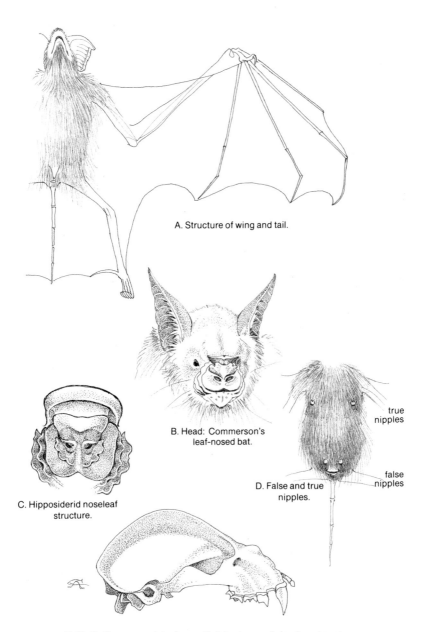

12

A. Structure of wing and tail.

B. Head: Commerson's
leaf-nosed bat.

C. Hipposiderid noseleaf
structure.

true
nipples

false
nipples

D. False and true
nipples.

E. Skull: Commerson's leaf-nosed bat, to show well-developed crest.

PERSIAN LEAF-NOSED BAT

Plate 12

(Persiese bladneusvlermuis)
Triaenops persicus

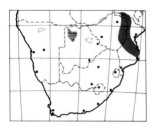

Total length about 14 cm; forearm: males 5,2 cm, females 5 cm; wingspan about 35 cm.

Known only from the northeastern parts of the Subregion, where it is common coastally, less so in the hinterland.

Colour varies from fawn brown to a bright cinnamon, but is usually yellowish brown; the underparts are lighter in shade than the upper. The small ears are deeply notched on their outside margins and have pointed tips.

They rest in caves or mine adits, in colonies of hundreds, in total darkness. A single young is born during the summer. **(S113)**

Order PRIMATES. Represented in the Subregion by three Families: the Lorisidae, Cercopithecidae and the Hominidae, man, of which only the first two are dealt with in this guide.

Family **LORISIDAE**. Represented in the Subregion by three species of bushbabies.

THICK-TAILED BUSHBABY

Plate 13
No. 2

(Bosnagaap)
Otolemur crassicaudatus

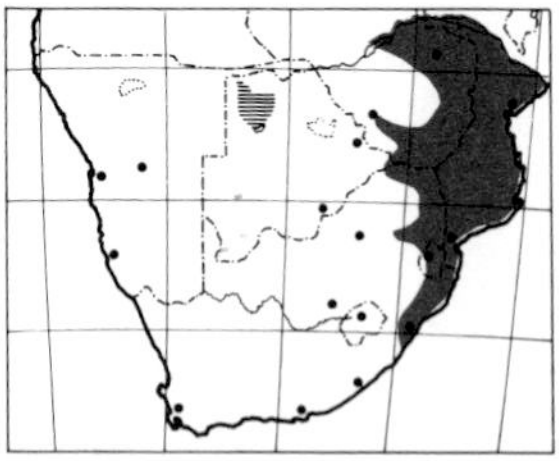

The largest of the three species; total length: males 74 cm, females 73 cm; tail: males 42 cm, females 41 cm.

Occurs only in the eastern and northeastern parts of the Subregion in forests and thickets.

Colour is pale grey, tinged brown or buffy, the fur long, fine and soft. The fluffy tail, which is longer than the head and body, may or may not have a dark tip. The head is small and rounded, the huge forwardly directed eyes ringed with a dark suffusion, the labile ears broad and rounded. There are five digits on the hands and feet, all armed with nails, except the second digits on the feet, which have a long, curved claw used in grooming.

Plate 13: 1. Lesser bushbaby (p. 44). **2.** Thick-tailed bushbaby (p. 42). **3.** Grant's lesser bushbaby (p. 45).

13

The thick-tailed bushbaby is nocturnal and arboreal and lives in small groups, foraging singly. The group rests during the day in the thick foliage of trees, the adult males often separate from the others. A number of these resting places may be scattered throughout the home range which is scent-marked with chest-gland secretion and urine dribbled onto the hands and feet and trodden onto branches. It is adept at climbing and jumping among the branches of trees, but is less agile on the ground, where it moves on all four feet or hops on the hind feet, holding the tail high. It lives on wild fruits and the gum exuding from trees, as well as on insects and occasionally reptiles and birds.

Litters of up to two are born during the summer months in the resting places, which are lined with fresh foliage. It is usually quiet, but can be very noisy, repeatedly calling with a loud harsh wailing, which can be heard over considerable distances. It also chatters and has a shrill alarm call. **(S114)**

LESSER BUSHBABY

(Nagapie)
Galago moholi

Plate 13
No. 1

Total length about 37 cm, tail about 22 cm.

Occurs only in the northern and northeastern parts of the Subregion in woodland.

Light grey in colour, or light grey washed with buffy or brown. The fluffy tail, which is longer than the head and body, often has a slightly darker tip. The head is small and rounded, with a short muzzle. The huge eyes are forwardly directed and the ears are rounded and extremely mobile. The five digits on the hands and feet are equipped with nails, except the second digits on the feet, which are armed with a curved claw used in grooming.

The lesser bushbaby is nocturnal and arboreal and lives in small family groups, foraging solitarily in a home range marked like those of the thick-tailed bushbaby. The group rests during the day in holes in trees, in platform-like nests in thick foliage or sometimes in disused birds' nests. It is at home among the branches of trees, climbing or leaping around with great agility, and less so on the ground, where it progresses in a series of hops on the hind feet or clambers on all four feet. It lives on a diet of gum from trees and on insects, catching the latter in its hands.

Up to two young are born in nests lined for their accommodation with fresh young leaves. The females may have two litters in the season, the first in the early summer and a second in the late summer; the higher proportion is in the later period. The females carry the young from the nest when foraging, parking them on a convenient branch while they feed. There is a wide repertoire of vocalisations, including a repeated *tchak-tchak,* which can rise in intensity to a noisy chattering; it also grunts, clicks and cackles and emits a warning moan. **(S115)**

GRANT'S LESSER BUSHBABY   Plate 13
(Grant se nagapie)   No. 3
Galagoides zanzibaricus

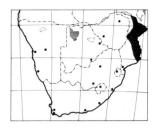

Slightly larger than the lesser bushbaby; total length 39 cm, tail 23 cm.

Found only in the extreme northeastern parts of the Subregion at low altitudes, where it lives in forest.

Distinctly browner in colour than the lesser bushbaby, with a longer rostrum.

It has more carnivorous tendencies than the lesser bushbaby, its call is harsher and more strident and persistent, and it tends to be more gregarious. Present indications are that up to two young are born during the summer months.   **(S116)**

Family **CERCOPITHECIDAE**. Represented in the Subregion by the chacma baboon and two species of monkey. All three are social by nature, the baboons intensely so, and they all live in troops. Their bodies are human-like in shape but, unlike man, in which the hind legs are longer than the arms, their limbs are subequal in length and they have long non-prehensile tails.

CHACMA BABOON   Plate 14
(Kaapse bobbejaan)   No. 3
Papio ursinus

Total length: males 1,5 m, females 1,2 m; mass: males up to 44 kg, females 17 kg.

Widespread in the Subregion, except in desert.

Colour varies greatly, depending on sex, age and origin, but is generally greyish brown or dark brown, sometimes nearly black; the females are usually lighter in colour than the males. Characteristically the long tail is carried with the proximal third held upwards, the distal two-thirds drooping downwards. They have horny epidermal callosities on their rumps which, in the males, fuse below the anus and, in the females, are separated in the middle by a wide space. The males have longer, better-developed muzzles and canine teeth than the females. A female's callosities are red and swollen when she is sexually receptive.

Diurnal; they live in troops numbering up to 100 individuals. They rest at night in krantzes or high trees and are omnivorous. A single dark haired young is born at any time during the year.

The adult males in the troops initiate and maintain their movements and figure prominently in the noisy and spectacular bouts of aggression and chasing among themselves and other members of the troops. Encounters between troops are often peaceful but fierce fighting may take place.

45

Stimulated by the approach of danger, the males vocalise with a loud bisyllabic bark, which can be heard over great distances, and members of troops scream and squeal when fighting. **(S117)**

VERVET MONKEY
(Blouaap)
Cercopithecus aethiops

Plate 14
No. 1

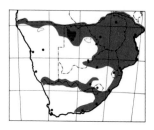

Total length: males up to 1,3 m, females 1 m; mean mass: males 5,5 kg, females 4 kg.

Occurs in the northeastern, eastern and southern parts of the Subregion and in the Orange and Vaal river valleys westwards in woodland.

The body is grey, the underparts and inner sides of the limbs white, the hair around the anus and base of the tail rufous. There is some variation in colour, depending on place of origin. In northern Namibia it is tinged yellow down the mid-back and the limbs are whitish, and in the northeast the back is reddish, darkening towards the base of the tail. The face is black with a white transverse band on the forehead, which extends downward on either side to the cheeks. The tail is about half the total length and has a diffused dark tip.

Vervet monkeys are diurnal and live in troops of up to about 20, which rest at night in the heavy foliage of high trees or sometimes in the shelter of rocky krantzes. They are vegetarians but have carnivorous tendencies and will take birds, eggs and chicks as well as insects. Food may be stored in the cheek pouches. They can become problem animals where grain crops and fruits are grown. A single dark-furred young, rarely twins, is born at any time of the year. They have a repertoire of at least 36 vocalisations, including six alarm calls, the intensity of the call reflecting the degree of stimulation. **(S119)**

SAMANGO MONKEY
(Samango-aap)
Cercopithecus mitis

Plate 14
No. 2

Total length: males 1,4 m, females 1,1 m; mean mass: males 9,3 kg, females 4,9 kg.

Occurs only in the eastern parts of the Subregion and is confined to a forest habitat.

Plate 14: 1. Vervet monkey (p. 46). **2.** Samango monkey (p. 46). **3.** Female and male Chacma baboons (p. 45).

1

2

3

Darker in colour than the vervet monkey, the shoulders, limbs and tail black, the back from the shoulders to the base of the tail suffused with reddish brown, the reddish colour intensifying towards the base of the tail. The throat is white, the underparts and insides of the limbs whitish or buffy white, the face dark brown.

These monkeys are diurnal and live in troops of up to 30, which rest at night in the thick foliage of tall trees. They feed on a wide range of ripe wild fruits, flowers, dry and green leaves, and will take insects and especially caterpillars, which are sought after. They raid orchards for fruits such as guavas, mangoes and bananas, but are not considered to be such a pest as the vervet monkey. A single young, rarely twins, is born early in the summer months. The adult males vocalise with a loud booming call during troop encounters. The most common call heard is the alarm call, a loud repeated *nyah*, but they also chuckle and the females and juveniles emit a high-pitched bird-like call when disturbed, or will squeal, chatter or scream. **(S120)**

Order PHOLIDOTA. This Order is represented in Africa by a single Family, the MANIDAE, one species of which, the pangolin, *Manis temminckii,* occurs in the Subregion.

PANGOLIN
(letermagô)
Manis temminckii

Plate 15
No. 3

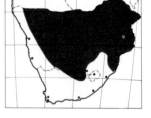

Total length about a metre, mass up to 15 kg.

Widely but sparsely distributed in the central and northern parts of the Subregion, occurring in a wide variety of types of habitat but not in forest or desert.

Immediately recognisable by its armour of heavy, imbricated, brown scales, which cover the upper parts of the body, and the small pointed head, which is partially covered with small scales. The underparts of the body lack scales and are thinly covered with curly hair. The tiny eyes are set in bulbous sockets; the ears lack pinnae and appear as small vertical slits in the sides of the head. There are five digits on the front feet; the first, the thumb, armed with a nail, the central three with long curved claws and the fifth with a short claw, and five digits on the rounded hind feet, each with a small nail-like claw. It has no teeth, but has a very long, sticky tongue, which, after it has opened up ants' nests or occasionally termite mounds with the claws, it inserts into the tunnels to capture the ants or termites on which it feeds. It is very powerful and under stress rolls up into a ball which has to be handled with care as the slicing movement of the tail can trap the fingers and inflict a deep cut.

Nocturnal and solitary, it walks on the hind feet, the tail held off the ground, the front of the long claws on the forefeet only occasionally touching it and then marking in the spoor. During the day it conceals itself in piles of leaves or other vegetable debris or in holes in the ground. A single young is born about June/July and, as it grows up, is carried by the female, clinging across the base of her tail. If disturbed, the female will roll into a ball enclosing the head and most of the body of the young. **(S121)**

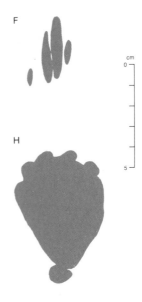

F

H

Order LAGOMORPHA. Represented in the Subregion by a single Family, the LEPORIDAE, which includes two hares, three red rock rabbits, the riverine rabbit and the introduced rabbit. The hares differ from the rabbits in features of their incisor teeth, their chromosome complement, morphology of the sperm and the development of the young at birth. The riverine rabbit is among the rarest of southern African mammals. The introduced rabbit survives only on offshore islands.

CAPE HARE
(Vlakhaas)
Lepus capensis

Plate 15
No. 2

Smaller and lighter in build than the scrub hare; total length 45–60 cm, mass 1,6–2,0 kg.

Widely distributed in the west and southwest of the Subregion and in localised areas in the north and east. Prefers more open country than the scrub hare, occurring on open grassland or grassland with a light scrub cover.

More variable in colour than the scrub hare. In the Cape Province the soft woolly fur on the upper parts of the body is light buffy in colour, finely speckled with black, the sides of the nose and cheeks tinged with yellow, the nuchal patch on the nape of the neck brownish pink, the underparts ochre-yellow and the abdomen pure white. In northeastern Botswana the colour is lighter; the upper parts of the body whitish grey, speckled with grey, the sides of the nose, cheeks and nuchal patch light grey, the underparts white or white with a narrow, indistinct ochre-yellow margin. In the Cape Province the fluffy tail is black above and white below; in northeastern Botswana the black is suffused and less distinct. The Cape hare has long, round-tipped ears fringed with short black or grey hair.

Nocturnal and solitary, it lies up during the day with its ears folded back on the body, in "forms" in the shelter of grass or bushes. These "forms" are characteristic in shape, the grass flattened by the fore and hind parts of the hare's body as it crouches in concealment. Under stress it will hide in holes in the ground, behaviour not recorded for the scrub hare. It lives on grass, preferring to feed where it is short and green. Young may be born at any time throughout the year, up to three constituting a litter. The young are fully haired at birth and capable of moving around on their own.   **(S122)**

SCRUB HARE
(Kolhaas)
Lepus saxatilis

Plate 15
No. 1

Varies in size; those from the southwestern Cape Province are the largest, the size decreasing northeastwards to Zimbabawe. Total length 50–60 cm, mass 2,0–4,5 kg.

Widespread in southern Africa, and is one of our commoner small mammals. Unlike the Cape hare, it tends to avoid the more open areas of grassland, preferring a habitat that affords more substantial cover of tall grass, bushes or scrub. The scrub hare is particularly common in agriculturally developed areas where the lands have a fringing cover of woodland, bushes or tall grass.

The upper parts of the body are covered with soft, woolly, greyish or buffy coloured fur, finely speckled with black; the underparts pure white. The fluffy tail is black above and white below, the nuchal patch orange-buffy. The ears of individuals from the southwestern Cape Province are very large, a characteristic feature of scrub hares from this area. The feet have long hair between the pads, which obliterates the marking of the pads in the spoor.

Nocturnal and solitary, it lies up like the Cape hare in "forms" during the day, with its ears folded back on its body. It lives on grass, preferring to feed

---

Plate 15:   **1.** Scrub hare (p. 50).   **2.** Cape hare (p. 49).   **3.** Pangolin (p. 48).

where it is fresh and green. The young are born at any time of the year, litters numbering up to three, more usually two. The young are fully haired at birth and capable of moving on their own. **(S123)**

Three species of **red rock rabbit** occur. They are associated with rocky terrain or boulder-strewn areas and are therefore discontinuous in occurrence. Nocturnal, they rest during the day deep in rock crevices. While they forage singly, a number may live together in restricted areas of rocky habitat. They are grazers and have litters of up to three young, which, unlike hares, are naked at birth and only leave the nests, which are lined with the mother's fur, when well grown.

SMITH'S RED ROCK RABBIT
(Smith se rooiklipkonyn)
Pronolagus rupestris

Plate 16
No. 3

The smallest of the three species; total length 53 cm, mean mass 1,6 kg.

Widespread in the southern parts of the Sub-region.

Colour varies, but is usually rufous brown grizzled with black; the rump and back legs are bright rufous, the sides of the face greyish, the underparts pinkish buff. The bushy tail is dark brown to rusty brown with a black tip and the nuchal patch is rufous.

Indications suggest that one or two young are born during the summer months in sheltered places under tree roots or rocks, in nests lined with the mother's fur. **(S124)**

NATAL RED ROCK RABBIT
(Natalse rooiklipkonyn)
Pronolagus crassicaudatus

Plate 16
No. 2

The largest of the three species; total length 57 cm, mean mass 2,6 kg.

Occurs only in Natal and marginally in parts of the adjacent provinces.

Plate 16: 1. Jameson's red rock rabbit (p. 54). **2.** Natal red rock rabbit (p. 52). **3.** Smith's red rock rabbit (p. 52). **4.** Riverine rabbit (p. 54).

16

The body is rufous brown, grizzled with black, the rump and back of the hind legs bright rufous, the underparts rufous buff and the forehead and sides of the face grey. The feature that distinguishes this species from the other two is the greyish white band that extends from the chin along the lower jaw and upwards to the nuchal patch, which varies in colour from brown to grey.

No information is available on reproduction in this species. **(S125)**

JAMESON'S RED ROCK RABBIT   Plate 16
(Jameson se rooiklipkonyn)   No. 1
Pronolagus randensis

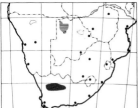

Total length 56 cm, mean mass 2,3 kg.

Occurs in two discrete areas, one in the northeast, the other in the northwest.

The upper parts of the body are rufous brown in colour, grizzled with black; the rump and back and the hind limbs are lighter in colour. The head is light grey flecked with brown, and contrasts with the colour of the body. The underparts are pinkish buff, the fluffy tail ochraceous brown with a black tip.

Indications suggest that one or two young are born at any time throughout the year in shelter in the rocky habitat. **(S126)**

RIVERINE RABBIT   Plate 16
(Rivierkonyn of oewerkonyn)   No. 4
Bunolagus monticularis

Total length 52 cm, mean mass 1,7 kg.

Distribution restricted to dense riverine scrub fringing seasonal rivers in the central Karoo.

The upper parts of the body are grey grizzled with black, the flanks tinged rufous, the chest and belly tinged yellow, the eyes ringed with yellow. The characteristic features that distinguish this species from other members of the Family are the diffused black band along the side of the lower jaw, which broadens out and disappears towards the base of the ear, the greyish bushy tail and the thick well-haired feet.

The species is endangered by the destruction of its habitat through cultivation.

Nocturnal and solitary, it lies up in forms during the day. Green grass is eaten in the summer and the leaves of shrubs in winter. Litters of one or two are born in shallow, fur-lined burrows throughout the year except in the coldest winter months. **(S127)**

RABBIT
(Konyn)
Oryctolagus cuniculus

First introduced by van Riebeeck about 1654 to Robben Island; this introduction, which was unsuccessful, was accompanied by an instruction from
the East India Company that they were not to be released on the mainland.
Several further introductions followed and by 1659 they were abundant on this
island. Other islands were subsequently stocked and, where there is sufficient
vegetation to support a population, they have flourished. Today seven of our
offshore islands support viable rabbit populations. Subsequently deliberate or
accidental releases have taken place on the mainland but predation and other
factors mitigate against their survival and they have died out.   **(S128)**

Order RODENTIA. The characteristic feature of all members of this Order is
their possession of pairs of ever-growing, chisel-like incisor teeth in the
upper and lower jaws, the points of which remain sharp through occlusion
between them. Between these teeth and the cheekteeth, which number
three or four (sometimes five) in each jaw half, there is a space (the
diastema), which can be closed by a flap of skin from the upper lips to allow
food to pass to the cheekteeth, which grind it up into a state suitable for
swallowing, or opened to allow inedible fragments to be ejected from the
sides of the mouth. Representatives of this Order occur throughout the
world; nine Families, comprising 78 species, four of them introduced, are
found in southern Africa.

Family **BATHYERGIDAE.** This Family is represented in the Subregion by three
genera and five species of molerats, which are in fact neither true moles nor
rats, but an assemblage of doubtful relationships. Endemic to Africa south of
the Sahara, all its members have reduced eyes and ear pinnae, short legs,
barely perceptible tails and powerful, ever-growing incisor teeth. They live
subterranean lives.

CAPE DUNE MOLERAT
(Kaapse duinmol)
Bathyergus suillus

Plate 17
No. 2

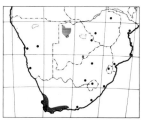

The largest of the molerats; total length: males
33 cm, females 30 cm, tail: males 5 cm, females
4,7 cm.
   Occurs only in the extreme southwestern

parts of the Cape Province, in sandy soil.

The body is light buffy in colour, the grey bases of the hair showing, giving it an uneven colour. Patches of whitish hair mark the position of the eyes and ear apertures and there is sometimes a white blaze on the forehead; the underparts are dark grey. The five digits on the feet are armed with long claws adapted to digging.

The burrows are up to about 20 cm in diameter and may extend up to 100 m in length, mounds of soil being thrown up in their excavation. They are occupied by groups of up to five individuals. This molerat lives on roots and bulbs and has litters of up to four young during the summer months. **(S129)**

NAMAQUA DUNE MOLERAT Plate 17
(Namakwa-duinmol) No. 3
Bathyergus janetta

Total length: males 25 cm, females 23 cm; tail: males about 5 cm, females 4,5 cm.

Occurs only in the northwestern Cape Province in sand dunes or sandy alluvium.

Varies in colour from drab grey to silvery grey, with a broad dark band down the mid-back from the neck to the rump. The eyes and ear openings are marked by patches of white hair. The underparts are dark grey. The head and face are suffused with black, often with a small white blaze on the forehead. The tail and sides of the hind feet are fringed with long, stiff bristles to assist in pushing loose soil out of the burrows.

Lives on roots and bulbs. Nothing is known of its reproduction. **(S130)**

COMMON MOLERAT Plate 17
(Vaalmol) No. 1
Cryptomys hottentotus

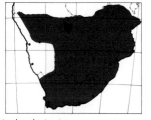

Total length 15 cm, tail about 2 cm.

Widespread throughout the Subregion, although there are no records at the moment from the greater part of southern Namibia. It burrows in most soil types, except heavy clay or hard compacted substrates.

Plate 17: 1. Common molerat (p. 56). **2.** Cape dune molerat (p. 55). **3.** Namaqua dune molerat (p. 56). **4.** Cape molerat (p. 58).

17

1

2

3

4

Colour varies from buff to slatey grey, the underparts lighter than the upper, and there is usually a small white blaze on the forehead, but this is by no means always present. The fur is short, soft and silky. The tail, which is fringed with long hair, is very short.

Small groups of up to about ten live in a burrow, throwing up mounds of excavated soil along its length, especially after rain. If the burrow is opened they are quick to close it with a plug of soil pushed into place with the hindquarters. They live on roots, bulbs and tubers and the underground stolons of grasses, and have litters of up to five young at any time of the year.

(S132)

Cryptomys damarensis is a newly-recognised species.

CAPE MOLERAT   Plate 17
(Kaapse blesmol)   No. 4
Georychus capensis

Total length about 20 cm, tail 3 cm.

Occurs in the southwestern parts of the Cape Province, in parts of southwestern Natal and southeastern Transvaal, in coastal sand dunes and sandy soils.

Buffy to orange-buffy in colour, some individuals distinctly reddish. Characteristic features are the black markings on the head, a white snout and chin and large patches of white surrounding the ear openings and the eyes and on the forehead. The flanks tend to be greyer and the hair of the underparts is grey at the base with broad white or buffy tips. The tail is very short for the size of the body.

Little is known about the habits of this molerat, except that it burrows shallowly and throws up mounds. It lives on bulbs, roots and tubers and can become a problem animal in vegetable gardens, taking potatoes and other root crops and young green vegetables. Nothing is known of the time at which the young are born or the number in litters, but there are indications from the appearance of very young individuals that they are born during the summer months.

(S133)

Family **HYSTRICIDAE**, the porcupine. Three species of porcupine occur in Africa: the brush-tailed porcupine in West and Central Africa; the crested porcupine in North, West and East Africa, and one in the Subregion.

PORCUPINE
(Ystervark)
Hystrix africaeaustralis

Plate 18
No. 4

Total length: males about 84 cm, females 86 cm; tail: males 13 cm, females 12 cm; mean mass: males 16,9 kg, females 18,4 kg.

Widespread throughout the Subregion.

Unmistakable among southern African mammals; the upper parts of the body from the shoulders to the tail are armed with long black-and-white pliable spines and stout, sharp quills which, when erected, effectively protect the body. There is a crest of long black-and-white bristly hair from the top of the head to the shoulders and the remainder of the body is clothed with coarse black, flattened hair, often with patches of white on either side of the base of the neck. The end of the tail is armed with a "rattle" of hollow-ended quills with narrow stalk-like bases.

The porcupine is nocturnal, foraging alone or in pairs and resting in caves, rock cavities or holes in the ground which are shared by family groups of up to six. When disturbed it will freeze, standing motionless, but if cornered can become aggressive, stamping its back feet, grunting and rattling its tail quills and suddenly rushing backwards onto its adversary to plant its sharp quills.

It lives on bulbs, tubers and roots, which it digs up, and will take wild fruits, bark and occasionally carrion. It can become a problem animal where agricultural crops such as groundnuts, potatoes and mealies are grown. Litters of up to three young are born in nests in the resting holes, lined with vegetable debris, during the summer months. **(S134)**

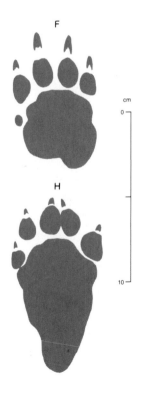

F

cm
0

H

10

59

Family **PEDETIDAE**. Represented by a single species, the springhaas, whose relationship has been widely debated.

SPRINGHAAS
(Springhaas)
Pedetes capensis

Plate 18
No. 1

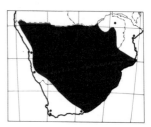

Total length about 80 cm, tail 43 cm.

Widespread in the Subregion, except in the southwest and extreme northern sectors, on sandy soils.

The hair on the body and tail is straight, long and soft. The colour of the body and proximal parts of the tail is reddish, the tip of the tail bushy and broadly black. The head is small and rounded, with upstanding pointed ears. The hind legs are much longer than the forelegs, giving a kangaroo-like appearance. The underparts of the body and tail are whitish or washed with yellow, except in the extreme northeastern parts of the range, where the under surface of the tail is black. There are five digits on the front feet, armed with strong, curved claws, and four on the hind, the third to fifth elongated and each digit armed with a broad, triangular, sharp-edged claw.

Nocturnal, it excavates burrows, the entrances with a ramp of soil thrown up in the excavation, with a resting chamber and an escape burrow leading up to the surface. Its eyes shine very brightly in a dazzling light at night. It lives on grass seed and the succulent underground stems of grass as well as corms, roots and rhizomes that it digs up with the curved claws on the front feet. A single young, rarely twins, is born in the burrows at any time of the year, in some parts with a peak in the late winter months. **(S135)**

Plate 18: 1. Springhaas (p. 60). 2. Woodland dormouse (p. 62). 3. Spectacled dormouse (p. 62). 4. Porcupine (p. 59).

18

Family **GLIRIDAE**, dormice. This Family is represented in the Subregion by four species. They have bushy tails like squirrels, soft, dense, greyish coloured fur, and four molar teeth, which distinguishes them from rats and mice, which have only three. They have four digits on the front feet, five on the hind feet, armed with curved claws.

SPECTACLED DORMOUSE Plate 18
(Gemsbokmuis) No. 3
Graphiurus ocularis

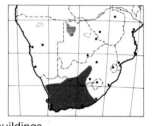

The largest of the dormice; total length: males 25 cm, females 23 cm; tail: males 11 cm, females 10 cm.
  Found only in the Cape Province, usually in rocky places, but will nest in trees, sheds and outbuildings.
  The upper parts of the body are silvery grey, the cheeks and chin white, with white patches above the ears, in front of the shoulders and on the flanks. Contrasting with these white markings, there is a black suffusion on the face from below the ears extending forwards through the eyes to the snout. The bushy tail is white-tipped, the underparts whitish.
  Nocturnal and to some extent arboreal, it lives on insects and seeds and in captivity will eat meat. Nothing is known about its reproduction. **(S136)**

WOODLAND DORMOUSE Plate 18
(Boswaaierstertmuis) No. 2
Graphiurus murinus

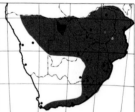

Total length 17 cm, tail 7 cm.
  Widespread, except in the more arid parts of the Subregion, in woodland and other shelter.
  Grey or buffy grey in colour, with a distinct dark suffusion around the eyes; the lower parts of the face and chin are white, the underparts greyish white, the fore and hind feet white, and the bushy tail greyish white with a white tip.
  Nocturnal and arboreal, it lives in holes in trees or under loose bark and commonly uses the shelter of the roofs of houses or outbuildings. Litters of up to three young are born in holes during the summer months. **(S138)**

Two other closely allied species occur, the **rock dormouse (S137)** and the **lesser savanna dormouse (S139),** the former slightly larger than the woodland dormouse, with a flattened skull allowing it to use narrow rock crevices; the latter the smallest of the dormice, whose status as a species remains uncertain.

Family **SCIURIDAE**. Represented in the Subregion by four genera and six species of indigenous ground and arboreal squirrels and one introduced species, the grey squirrel. All the members have bushy tails, the ground squirrels being characterised by their short, bristly hair.

GROUND SQUIRREL   Plate 19
(Waaierstertgrondeekhoring)   No. 5
Xerus inauris

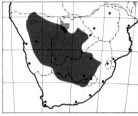

Total length 45 cm, tail 21 cm.
    Occurs only in the drier areas of the central and western parts of the Subregion in open country, on hard ground with some scrub cover.
    Cinnamon in colour, some darker, some lighter; the lower part of the limbs, the underparts and the sides of the neck white. The characteristic features are the bushy tail, the white stripe on the flanks from the shoulders to the thighs, the white rings around the eyes and the coat of short bristly hair. There are four digits on the front feet and five on the hind, armed with long, sharp claws adapted to digging. The slit-like nostrils can be closed at will when burrowing.
    Diurnal and gregarious, they live in colonies numbering up to 30, in warrens with resting chambers. The males move around between the colonies, which are dominated by a female. They are predominantly vegetarian, but will eat insects. Litters of up to three young are born in the warrens at any time throughout the year.   **(S140)**

    The closely allied **mountain ground squirrel (S141)** differs in having orange-yellow incisor teeth and larger eye orbits, and occurs only in rocky parts of Namibia. It vocalises with a high-pitched whistle. Both species growl or scream when thoroughly alarmed.

SUN SQUIRREL   Plate 19
(Soneekhoring)   No. 1
Heliosciurus mutabilis

A large squirrel; total length 50 cm, tail 27 cm.
    Occurs in forests in the northeastern parts of the Subregion.
    The colour of the body is usually light brown, but varies greatly, one subspecies from eastern Zimbabwe being black. Further variation is produced by the moult, the old hair foxing to reddish, with a clear line of division marking the moult. The underparts also vary from white to brownish or yellowish brown.

Diurnal and usually solitary, it rests in holes in trees or among tangled creepers. It is predominantly vegetarian but will take insects. Indications are that litters of up to four young are born during the summer months. When alarmed it clucks loudly, flicking its tail. **(S142)**

STRIPED TREE SQUIRREL Plate 19
(Gestreepte boomeekhoring) No. 2
Funisciurus congicus

A small species; total length 32 cm, tail 17 cm.

Occurs only in northwestern Namibia, in woodland.

Buffy yellow in colour and characterised by a longitudinal white stripe, bordered below with a black suffusion, on the flanks. The underparts are white tinged with yellow towards the anus.

Diurnal and arboreal, it forages on the ground as well as in the trees and is predominantly vegetarian, living on seeds, nuts and wild fruits, but will also take insects. Litters of two young are born during the summer months in holes in trees; females sometimes have two litters in a season. Vocalisation takes the form of bird-like chirps, or high-pitched chattering accompanied by tail flicking. **(S143)**

RED SQUIRREL Plate 19
(Rooi eekhoring) No. 4
Paraxerus palliatus

Total length about 40 cm, tail about 20 cm.

Occurs only in forest in the eastern and northeastern parts of the Subregion.

Colour varies greatly, depending on place of origin, the upper parts of the body varying from a grizzled dark grey to a grizzled black. The underparts, sides of the face and the tail are either reddish, yellowish or auburn, these bright colours serving to distinguish them from other squirrels.

Diurnal, resting in holes in trees or in thick matted creepers. Predominantly vegetarian, it lives on nuts, berries, wild fruits, leaves and flowers and will take insects. Litters of up to two are born in leaf-lined holes in trees during the

---

Plate 19: 1. Sun squirrel (p. 63). **2.** Striped tree squirrel (p. 64). **3.** Tree squirrel (p. 66). **4.** Red squirrel (p. 64). **5.** Ground squirrel (p. 63).

summer months. Vocalisation takes the form of clicking, which rises in intensity with the degree of stress, as well as murmuring, growling and hissing.

(S144)

TREE SQUIRREL ✓
(Boomeekhoring)
Paraxerus cepapi

Plate 19
No. 3

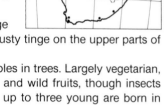

Total length about 35 cm, tail about 17 cm.
Widespread in woodland in the northeastern parts of the Subregion.
Pale grey in colour in the west of its range and buffy in the east, in parts with a distinct rusty tinge on the upper parts of the limbs and head.

It is diurnal and forages singly, resting in holes in trees. Largely vegetarian, living on flowers, leaves, seeds, berries, bark and wild fruits, though insects form an important part of the diet. Litters of up to three young are born in holes in trees at any time throughout the year, with a peak during summer. It vocalises with clicks and a harsh rattle, which rises in intensity as its alarm increases, this latter sound accompanied by tail flicking.   **(S145)**

GREY SQUIRREL
(Gryseekhoring)
Sciurus carolinensis

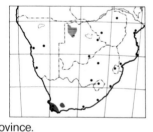

A large species; total length: males 46 cm, females 48 cm; tail: males 20 cm, females 22 cm.
Introduced by Cecil Rhodes to Groote Schuur Estate, Cape Town, about the turn of the century and has become feral in the southwestern Cape Province.

Colour is silvery grey to yellowish brown, depending on the time of the year.
The grey squirrel lives on acorns, pine seeds and orchard fruits and will take birds' eggs and young vegetables. Litters of up to four are born in holes in trees, or "dreys", about the size of a football, made of twigs and leaves, during the summer months.   **(S146)**

Family **THRYONOMYIDAE**, canerats. Represented in the Subregion by two species, which differ in size and in the configuration of the grooves on the upper incisor teeth.

GREATER CANERAT

(Groot rietrot)

Thryonomys swinderianus

Plate 20

No. 3

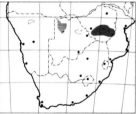

Total length: males 72 cm, females 67 cm; tail: males 19 cm, females 18 cm.

Occurs in the northern, northeastern and eastern parts of the Subregion, in reed beds and other rank vegetation fringing rivers, lakes and swamps. The growing of sugar cane and other agricultural crops has greatly improved the habitat for canerats in many parts of their range.

The body is short and stocky, with a short tail, and covered with a coat of spiny hair, which is speckled dark brown in colour and may be distinctly rusty tinged around the base of the tail. The underparts are whitish or greyish white, the small rounded ears almost obscured by the bristly hair. The front of the nose protrudes in front of the nostrils, acting like a pad when they butt each other with their noses. The grooves on the incisor teeth are situated near the inside edges of the teeth (in the lesser canerat they are more evenly spaced on the front surface).

Predominantly nocturnal and solitary, it rests in dense, rank vegetation or reed beds, and establishes runs to its feeding grounds, which are marked by the cut stems of grasses lying in small piles, and scattered piles of scats. When disturbed it may freeze until the danger passes and is difficult to dislodge from cover. Litters of up to three young are born in the cover of thick vegetation during the summer months. **(S147)**

LESSER CANERAT

(Klein rietrot)

Thryonomys gregorianus

Plate 20

No. 2

Much smaller than the greater canerat; total length 52 cm; tail: males 14 cm, females 13 cm.

So far, has only been shown to occur in southeastern Zimbabwe, where it occupies the same type of habitat as the greater canerat, but may also occupy much drier terrain, occurring even on dry rocky hillsides.

Similar to the greater canerat in appearance, apart from being much smaller. The differences lie in the incisor teeth, where the grooves on the front are much more evenly spaced than in the greater canerat, and the skull is slightly different in shape.

Nocturnal and usually solitary foragers, they live in family groups in restricted areas where there is a good grass cover. They use the cover of thick grass but will also rest in rock crevices. They form runs to their feeding grounds, which, like those of the greater canerat, are marked by piles of the cut stems of grasses on which they feed. Few records of breeding are available but the indications are that they have litters of up to three young late in summer or in early winter. **(S148)**

Family **PETROMURIDAE**. The dassie rat is the only representative of this Family.

DASSIE RAT   Plate 20
(Dassierot)   No. 1
Petromys typicus

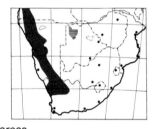

Total length: males 31 cm, females 29 cm; tail 14 cm.
   Occurs only in the western parts of the Subregion, its distribution extending marginally into southwestern Angola, where it lives in rocky areas.
   Squirrel-like in appearance, but lacking a bushy tail. Colour varies from a grizzled grey to dark chocolate, some individuals nearly black; the underparts vary from white to yellow. The cheekteeth are unique in having such deep, oblique infoldings as to appear laminate. The skull is broad and flat, to allow the use of narrow rock crevices.
   Diurnal, they live in family groups, often sunning themselves in sheltered corners. They are fleet-footed and jump from rock to rock with agility, their tails trailing behind them. They are vegetarians and live on the leaves, stems and flowering heads of grasses, wild fruits and leaves. Litters of two young are born in rock crevices lined with dry leaves during the summer. **(S149)**

Families **CRICETIDAE** and **MURIDAE**, rats and mice. These two Families are usually dealt with together, as there are no clearcut characters to differentiate them, except the shape of the molar teeth. They include all the small mammals generally referred to as rats or mice, between which it is a matter of choice as to which name is applied. Usually the larger species are called rats, the smaller species mice, with no clear dividing line.

Plate 20:   **1.** Dassie rat (p. 68).   **2.** Lesser canerat (p. 67).   **3.** Greater canerat (p. 67).

20

BRANTS' WHISTLING RAT
(Brants se fluitrot)
Parotomys brantsii

Plate 21
No. 2

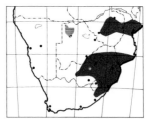

Total length 24 cm, tail 9 cm.

Occurs in the southwestern parts of the Subregion on dry, sandy ground.

Colour may vary from pale rusty yellow with whitish underparts and unicoloured tail in the southern Kalahari, to pale brownish yellow with greyish underparts in the southern areas, where the noticeably short tail is distinctly darker above than below. The hair is long, soft and woolly, the individual hairs with grey bases.

Diurnal, they are active in the early morning and often sit sunning themselves at the burrow entrances. If alarmed they vocalise with a sharp, piercing whistle and stamp their hind feet before diving for safety. The burrows have chambers lined with vegetable debris. They live on the stems and leaves of succulent plants as well as seeds. Litters of up to three young are born in the burrows during the summer months. **(S150)**

A closely allied species, **Littledale's whistling rat (S151)**, differs in the size of the ear bullae and has grooved incisor teeth, but is similar in habits. It is confined to the northwestern Cape Province and adjacent parts of Namibia.

ANGONI VLEI RAT
(Angoni-vleirot)
Otomys angoniensis

Plate 21
No. 4

Total length 30 cm, tail 8 cm.

Occurs in the eastern and northeastern parts of the Subregion, and is associated with wet vleis, swamps and swampy areas along rivers.

The colour of the body varies from pale to dark buff, the long, soft hair slate grey at the base with buffy tips. Characteristic features are the large ears and very short tail, barely a quarter of the total length, which is black above and pale buffy below. The hair of the underparts is dark grey at the base with buffy tips, giving an overall greyish appearance.

Diurnal, it builds domed grass nests in tussock grass above water level and forms well-defined runs to its feeding grounds, which are marked by small

---

Plate 21: **1.** Sloggett's rat (p. 72). **2.** Brant's whistling rat (p. 70). **3.** Vlei rat (p. 72). **4.** Angoni vlei rat (p. 70).

70

piles of discarded stems of grass, which is its principal food. Litters of up to four young are born during the summer months. **(S153)**

A similar but much larger rat, the **large vlei rat (S154)**, is found in the northern parts of the Subregion in similar habitat. It is now considered to be simply a subspecies of *O. angoniensis*.

VLEI RAT
(Vleirot)
Otomys irroratus

Plate 21
No. 3

Total length 24 cm, tail 9 cm.
   Widespread in the southern parts of the Subregion, north to the Transvaal and eastern Zimbabwe, in habitat similar to that of the Angoni vlei rat, but with a tendency to inhabit drier ground.
   The colour of the body is dark slate grey tinged with buff, the underparts paler and greyer. The tail is noticeably short, slightly over a third of the total length. It is difficult to distinguish from the Angoni vlei rat except by characters of the ear bullae and laminations of the cheekteeth.
   Diurnal, with habits similar to those of the Angoni vlei rat. Litters of up to seven young are born in the nests during the summer months. **(S156)**

Three other species of vlei rats occur in the Subregion: the **laminate vlei rat (S152)** in the east, with a relict population in the southwestern Cape Province; **Saunders' vlei rat (S155)** in the southern Cape Province and the **Karoo bushrat (S158)**, which lives in karroid areas in the southern Cape Province and prefers a drier habitat than other vlei rats. These differ in the number of laminations on the cheekteeth, but are difficult to identify with certainty by external examination alone.

SLOGGETT'S RAT
(Sloggett se rot)
Otomys sloggetti

Plate 21
No. 1

Total length 20 cm, tail 6 cm.
   Occurs in the eastern Cape Province and Drakensberg Mountains in Lesotho. It inhabits the highest altitude in the Subregion, the summit of Mont-aux-Sources at 3 282 m, and has, from its association with snow and ice, been called the ice rat.

The hair is long, soft and woolly, the body vinaceous brown, the flanks paler and greyer, the underparts buffy grey. The tail is dark above, buffy below and very short, about a quarter of the total length. The sides of the face and nose are rusty coloured, the ears noticeably small.

Diurnal, it suns itself on open vantage points in the morning and, after foraging for leaves and flowers, returns to the shelter of rock crevices or piles of boulders in the late afternoon. One or two young are born in spring and summer. **(S157)**

GROOVED-TOOTHED MOUSE
(Groeftandmuis)
Pelomys fallax

Plate 22
No. 3

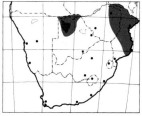

Total length 29 cm, tail 15 cm.

Occurs in the north and northeast of the Subregion and is associated with dry ground on the fringes of rivers or swamps.

Rusty brown to tawny yellow in colour, the coat with a distinct green or blue sheen, and grizzled with black. There is usually an indistinct diffused dark stripe down the mid-back. In some individuals the rump is rustier in colour than the remainder of the body. The underparts are off-white or light buffy brown, the tail black on top, buffy or white below.

Predominantly nocturnal, but is active in the early morning. It burrows in dry ground adjacent to wet areas and lives on green vegetable matter and seeds. Litters of up to four young are born in the burrows during the summer months. **(S159)**

SPINY MOUSE
(Stekelmuis)
Acomys spinosissimus

Plate 22
No. 1

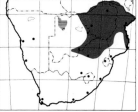

Total length 17 cm, tail about 9 cm.

Widespread in the northeastern parts of the Subregion, and is associated with rocky areas.

Its most characteristic feature is its spiny coat, which distinguishes it from other murids. The summer coat is sepia grey, foxing to reddish during the winter, the underparts pure white.

Nocturnal, it rests in rock crevices or under tree roots and lives on grass and other seeds, but will also take insects and small invertebrates. Litters of up to five young are born during the summer months. **(S160)**

A closely allied species, the **Cape spiny mouse (S161),** occurs in the south-western Cape Province in rocky areas.

SINGLE-STRIPED MOUSE
(Eenstreepmuis)
Lemniscomys rosalia

Plate 22
No. 4

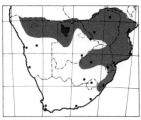

Total length 27 cm, tail 15 cm.

Occurs in the northern and northeastern parts of the Subregion in grassland.

Colour varies greatly, from pale vinaceous buff in the drier areas to reddish orange in the higher rainfall areas, but this mouse is everywhere characterised by the clearly marked dark stripe down the mid-back. The underparts are rusty white, the tail with a dark or rusty coloured longitudinal stripe on top and white underneath.

Nocturnal, it excavates burrows under the cover of matted grass and lives on seed. Litters of up to five young are born in the burrows during the summer months. **(S162)**

STRIPED MOUSE
(Streepmuis)
Rhabdomys pumilio

Plate 22
No. 2

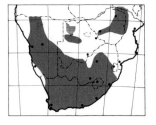

Total length varies geographically from 19 to 21 cm, tail 9–11 cm.

Widespread in the southern parts of the Subregion and in isolated areas northwards, where there is grass cover.

Varies in colour from pale reddish brown in the west to dark greyish buff in the east, but is everywhere characterised by the four distinct longitudinal stripes on the back, which clearly distinguish it from other murids. The underparts are white, the back of the ears reddish brown or yellowish brown, the tail darker above than below.

Diurnal, excavating burrows with entrances under clumps of grass, the chambers lined with soft vegetable debris. They enter houses freely and in parts have become commensal with man. They eat seeds, insects and soft, succulent vegetable matter, including the basal bracts and styles of protea flowers, and so become important agents in pollination. Litters of up to nine young are born in the burrows during the summer months. **(S163)**

Plate 22: 1. Spiny mouse (p. 73).   **2.** Striped mouse (p. 74).   **3.** Grooved-toothed mouse (p. 73).   **4.** Single-striped mouse (p. 74).   **5.** Woosnam's desert rat (p. 76).

22

WOOSNAM'S DESERT RAT
(Woosnam se woestynrot)
Zelotomys woosnami

Plate 22
No. 5

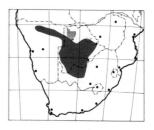

Total length 24 cm, tail 11 cm.

Confined in distribution to parts of the northern sector of the Subregion, where it occurs on Kalahari sand with a sparse cover of grass or scrub.

The body is pale smoke grey pencilled with black, the flanks paler, the underparts creamy white. The tail and feet are white.

A nocturnal species, excavating burrows in sandy soil or using those of other murids, particularly gerbils. They live on seeds and insects and have carnivorous tendencies, as gerbil hair has been found in their stomachs. Litters of up to 11 young (but more usually five) are born in the burrows during the summer months. **(S164)**

WATER RAT
(Waterrot)
Dasymys incomtus

Plate 23
No. 5

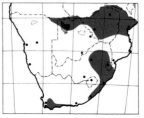

Total length 33 cm, tail 16 cm.

Distribution is discontinuous, from the southwestern Cape Province to the eastern and northeastern parts of the Subregion. The water rat is associated with wet conditions, living in reed beds, among semi-aquatic grasses in swampy areas or in wet vleis.

The colour is dark brown, the coat grizzled with buffy; the hair of the underparts is white-tipped, giving it a lighter colour than the upper parts. It has long, woolly hair, a relatively short tail, less than half the total length, large ears and dark feet with whitish claws.

The water rat is active in the early morning and late evening and forms runs, which are often shallowly inundated. It constructs domed grass nests in tussock grass with an entrance on the lower side above water level. It lives on the succulent fresh stems of grasses and will take insects. Litters of up to nine young are born during the summer months. **(S165)**

Plate 23: **1.** Woodland mouse (p. 78). **2.** House mouse (p. 78). **3.** Pygmy mouse (p. 79). **4.** Rudd's mouse (p. 79). **5.** Water rat (p. 76).

23

WOODLAND MOUSE

Plate 23
No. 1

(Woudmuis)

Grammomys dolichurus

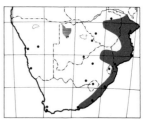

Total length 27 cm, tail 17 cm.

Occurs only in the eastern and northeastern parts of the Subregion in forests and thickets, usually in damp places.

The colour is tawny red, often distinctly redder on the rump, or may be tinged grey or totally grey. The underparts are pure white and sharply demarcated from the colour of the upper parts. The tail is noticeably long and thin, well over half the total length.

Nocturnal and predominantly arboreal, it constructs nests of grass or leaves in dense underbrush or will use weaver bird nests. It lives on green vegetable matter and wild fruits. Litters of up to four young are born at widely varying times of the year. **(S167)**

A closely allied species, the **Mozambique woodland mouse (S166)**, has patches of white hair at the base of the ears, and occurs on the same ground as this species.

HOUSE MOUSE

Plate 23
No. 2

(Huismuis)

Mus domesticus

Total length 16 cm, tail 9 cm.

This is an introduced species, which is widespread in the southern parts of the Subregion and in parts of the northeast wherever there are human dwellings. It has been transported widely throughout the world and is as much at home on Subantarctic islands as it is in temperate climates.

Colour is buffy brown, the underparts slightly lighter, the tail brown above and lighter brown below, the feet light buffy brown.

Nocturnal; it nests in any secluded cover, dragging in soft material for the lining. It is omnivorous, and can be destructive where there are stored foodstuffs. Litters of up to 13 young are born at any time throughout the year.

(S168)

PYGMY MOUSE
(Dwergmuis)
Mus minutoides

Plate 23
No. 3

A tiny mouse, with an adult mass of 5-6 g; total length 10 cm, tail 4,5 cm.

Widespread in the southern, eastern and northeastern parts of the Subregion, in a variety of types of habitat.

Varies greatly in colour from brownish buff to reddish, with pure white underparts. It has a relatively short tail, much shorter in the northeast than in the southwest.

Nocturnal; it either excavates its own burrows or uses other shelter. Its food is grass seed, green vegetable matter and insects. Litters of up to eight young are born during the summer months. **(S172)**

Setzer's pygmy mouse (S169) occurs only in parts of Botswana; the **grey-bellied pygmy mouse (S170)** marginally in the extreme northeast of the Subregion, and the **desert pygmy mouse (S171)** in parts of Botswana. These three species are little known and their relationships require clarification. **Thomas' pygmy mouse** has recently been recorded from Zimbabwe and Mozambique.

RUDD'S MOUSE
(Rudd se muis)
Uranomys ruddi

Plate 23
No. 4

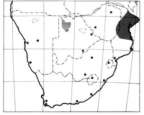

Total length about 15 cm, tail about 5 cm.

A rare species, found only in the extreme northeast of the Subregion on floodplain or grassland, in the vicinity of rivers.

Colour varies from light brown to grey, the flanks and underparts paler. The hair is long and springy in texture, each hair like a fine bristle. The coat has a distinct sheen.

Nocturnal; nothing is known about its habits or reproduction in the Subregion. In Malawi it is recorded as being insectivorous. **(S173)**

MULTIMAMMATE MOUSE

Plate 24
No. 3

(Vaal veldmuis)

Mastomys natalensis and *Mastomys coucha*

Total length 24 cm, tail 11 cm.

These two species are considered together as they are indistinguishable in the field and differ only in genetics, behaviour, blood proteins and certain skull characters only made apparent by multivariate analysis.

Widespread in the eastern and northern parts of the Subregion and in riverine associations running westwards into arid country. They are two of the commonest murid species and have become commensal with man.

The upper parts of the body vary in colour from light to dark grey, often suffused with black. The flanks are paler and tinged yellow or fawn. The hair of the underparts is grey at the base with narrow white tips, giving an overall dark grey appearance. The tail is finely scaled and sparsely covered with short hair, and is darker on the top than underneath. Each of the mammae of the females, up to 12 pairs, is surrounded by lighter hair, which marks them from the general grey colour of the underparts.

Nocturnal, they make nests lined with soft debris in sheltered places or will dig their own burrows. They are omnivorous, and can be problem animals where foodstuffs are stored. Litters of up to about 20 young are born at any time of the year. The females produce litters, under favourable conditions, at 33-day intervals. They can carry plague-infected fleas from veld rodents to man. **(S174)**

The closely allied **Shortridge's mouse (S175)** occurs only in the extreme northern parts of Botswana and Namibia, and **Verreaux's mouse (S176)** in the southwestern Cape Province.

TREE MOUSE

Plate 24
No. 1

(Boommuis)

Thallomys paedulcus

Total length about 30 cm, tail 16 cm.

Occurs in the northern and eastern parts of the Subregion in woodland, particularly *Acacia* woodland.

Colour is grey, tinged with yellow. The flanks are whitish grey, the underparts pure white. The head is pale grey, the eyes ringed with black, which extends forwards to the nostrils. The tail in western populations is black for the terminal two-thirds of its length, with a small tuft of black hair on the tip.

Nocturnal, it lives in holes in trees, packed with nesting material of vegetable debris, and feeds on the fine, fresh leaflets of thornbush, other green vegetation and insects. Litters of up to five young are born in the nests during the summer months. **(S177)**

NAMAQUA ROCK MOUSE   Plate 24
(Namakwalandse klipmuis)   No. 2
Aethomys namaquensis

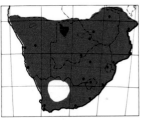

Total length 26 cm, tail 15 cm.
   Widespread throughout the Subregion in rocky areas, where it lives in rock crevices or, if these are not available, in trees or under bushes.
   Colour varies, but is generally reddish brown to yellowish brown, sometimes with a profuse admixture of black hairs, giving a darker appearance. The underparts are pure white or some of the hairs are grey-based, giving a slightly grey appearance. The tail is noticeably long, especially in northern populations, and is finely scaled.
   Nocturnal; it collects vegetable debris for the nest, huge piles of which mark its presence in rock crevices, holes in trees or under bushes. It lives on grass seed. Litters of up to seven young are born in the nests during the summer months. **(S179)**

   The closely allied **Grant's rock mouse (S180)** occurs only in the southern central parts of the Cape Province and is generally darker grey in colour, with a broader muzzle and heavier head.

RED VELD RAT   Plate 24
(Afrikaanse bosrot)   No. 4
Aethomys chrysophilus

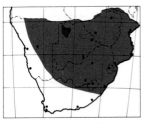

More heavily built than the Namaqua rock mouse; total length 30 cm, tail 15 cm.
   Widespread in the more northerly parts of the Subregion, with a wide habitat tolerance.
   Colour varies, but is usually in shades of reddish fawn, the flanks lighter in colour than the upper parts. The hairs of the underparts are basally grey with white tips, imparting an overall light grey colour. The tail is thicker and more coarsely scaled than that of the Namaqua rock mouse.
   Nocturnal, it burrows under bushes or will use existing holes or rock crevices. It lives on seed, and its large size also allows it to deal with hard shelled nuts. Litters of up to six young are born in the nests at any time throughout the year. **(S181)**

   A closely allied species, the **Silinda rat (S178)**, is only known from a few localities in eastern Zimbabwe and adjacent parts of Mozambique, and the

Nyika veld rat (S182) from the same area. They differ from the red veld rat in characters of the teeth.

HOUSE RAT	Plate 24
(Huisrot)	No. 5
Rattus rattus	

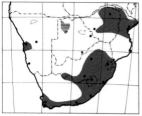

Total length 37 cm, tail 20 cm.

An introduced species, which has spread widely in the Subregion wherever there are human activities.

The house rat occurs in various shades of grey, the underparts either grey or white. The feet are heavier than those of any indigenous murid of similar size. The tail is about half the total length and heavily scaled.

The house rat is nocturnal, and nests in any substantial cover, pulling in any soft material to line the nest. It is omnivorous, and is inclined to sharpen its teeth by gnawing on hard materials and to cut holes in woodwork, and is a serious pest wherever it occurs. The white-bellied form tends to be more vegetarian in its diet. Litters of up to ten young are born at any time throughout the year and females produce up to six litters a year. **(S183)**

The closely allied **Norwegian or brown rat (S184)** occurs in ports but has not colonised the hinterland. These two rats originally brought plague-carrying fleas in southern Africa.

Gerbils resemble tiny kangaroos, their hind legs being longer and better developed than their forelegs, and unlike most other murids, their incisor teeth have a longitudinal groove on the front. They are of medical importance as some of them are a reservoir of the bacillus of plague that is endemic in parts of the subregion.

SHORT-TAILED GERBIL	Plate 25
(Kortstertnagmuis)	No. 2
Desmodillus auricularis	

Total length 20 cm, tail 9 cm.

Occurs in the drier western areas of the Subregion, on hard ground with a short grass or karroid bush cover.

Plate 24: 1. Tree mouse (p. 80). **2.** Namaqua rock mouse (p. 81). **3.** Multimammate mouse (p. 80). **4.** Red veld rat (p. 81). **5.** House rat (p. 82).

24

Variable in colour; individuals may be brownish buff, cinnamon buff, grey-brown or reddish brown, but all are characterised by the distinct white patches at the base of the ears and by their short tails, which are barely half the total length.

Nocturnal, living in complicated and extensive burrow systems with entrances under grass clumps or low bushes. It is a seed-eater, tending to carry the food back to the burrow entrances to be eaten. Litters of up to seven young are born in the burrows at any time throughout the year.   **(S185)**

HAIRY-FOOTED GERBIL   Plate 25
(Haarpootnagmuis)   No. 4
Gerbillurus paeba

A small species; total length 21 cm, tail 11 cm.

Widespread in the western parts of the Sub-region, with a narrow extension eastwards into southern Mozambique. It prefers substrate with some bush or grass cover.

Colour varies from reddish orange to greyish red, the underparts pure white. The tail is about half the total length and dark along the top.

Nocturnal, living in burrows with nesting chambers lined with vegetable debris and feeding on seeds and insects. Litters of up to five young are born in nests at any time throughout the year.   **(S186)**

Three other species of hairy-footed gerbils occur: the **dune hairy-footed gerbil (S187),** which is found in sand dunes in the Namib Desert; the **brush-tailed hairy-footed gerbil (S188),** which is found in the northwestern Cape Province and Namibia, and **Setzer's hairy-footed gerbil (S189)**, in the Namib Desert. The hairy feet of these gerbils are an adaptation to living on a loose, sandy substrate.

BUSHVELD GERBIL   Plate 25
(Bosveldse nagmuis)   No. 3
Tatera leucogaster

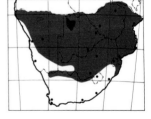

A large species; total length 28 cm, tail 15 cm.

Widespread in the northern parts of the Subregion on light sandy soils or sandy alluvium.

Colour varies from orange-buff to reddish

Plate 25: 1. Cape gerbil (p. 86). **2.** Short-tailed gerbil (p. 82). **3.** Bushveld gerbil (p. 84). **4.** Hairy-footed gerbil (p. 84). **5.** Gorongoza gerbil (p. 87).

brown; the western populations are lighter in colour than the eastern. The unscaled tail has a distinct dark suffusion on top for most of its length and is about half the total length.

Nocturnal, excavating burrows, the entrances of which are under low bushes and are characterised by the ramp of fresh soil thrown out nightly. The burrows have resting chambers floored with vegetable debris. It eats green vegetable matter, grass and other seeds, and insects. Litters of up to nine young are born in the nests, usually during the summer, but with births throughout the year. **(S190)**

CAPE GERBIL
(Kaapse nagmuis)
Tatera afra

Plate 25
No. 1

A large species; total length 30 cm, tail 15 cm.

Distribution is restricted to the extreme south-western parts of the Cape Province.

The body colour is variable and may be reddish orange or pale buffy, liberally but irregularly washed with dark brown, with pure white underparts. The Cape gerbil has large ears, and the tail is about half the total length. It has noticeably long, soft woolly fur, much longer than in other gerbils.

Nocturnal, excavating burrow systems in sandy soil, with chambers floored with vegetable debris. Litters of up to about six young are born in the burrows during the summer months. **(S191)**

HIGHVELD GERBIL
(Hoëveldse nagmuis)
Tatera brantsii

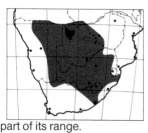

Total length about 28 cm, tail about 14 cm.

Widespread in the central parts of the Sub-region, on sandy soils or sandy alluvium, with some grass or scrub cover. It occurs on the same ground as the bushveld gerbil in the greater part of its range.

The colour of the body varies from light rufous brown to pale reddish with a wash of brown; populations in the eastern parts of their range are the darkest in colour. The underparts are pure white or buffy grey. The tail is the same colour as the body at its base but is irregularly pure white towards the tip, which is a useful character in identification. The fur is long, soft and woolly, but not as long as in the Cape gerbil.

Nocturnal; its burrow excavations are similar to those of the bushveld gerbil.

It lives on grass and other seeds, and insects. Litters of up to five young are born in the burrows at any time throughout the year. **(S192)**

The **Gorongoza gerbil (S193)** occurs only in eastern Zimbabwe and adjacent parts of Mozambique and is larger and darker in colour than the other species. (See Pl. 25, No. 5).

PYGMY ROCK MOUSE
(Dwergklipmuis)
Petromyscus collinus

Plate 26
No. 1

Total length: males 19,8 cm, females 16,8 cm; tail: males 9,5 cm, females 8,6 cm.

Found only in rocky areas in the western parts of the Subregion.

The body is grey tinged with yellow, sometimes reddish yellow. The hair of the underparts is grey at the base, with broad white tips, the feet greyish, the tail about half the total length.

Nothing is known about the diet of this species. Litters of up to three young are born during the summer months. **(S206)**

Another closely allied species, the **Brukkaros pygmy rock mouse (S205)**, is brownish buff in colour with grey underparts. It has a shorter tail and ears than the pygmy rock mouse and occurs in the northwestern Cape Province and southern Namibia.

WHITE-TAILED MOUSE
(Witstertmuis)
Mystromys albicaudatus

Plate 26
No. 3

Total length: males 22 cm, females 21 cm; tail about 6 cm.

Occurs in the southwestern and southeastern parts of the Subregion in grassland, karroo areas and *fynbos*.

It is thickset in build, with a large head and soft, woolly coat. The body is light grey or buffy grey, with a pencilling of black. The hair of the underparts is grey at the base with light grey or white tips. The tail, which is barely a third of the total length, is white and sparsely haired. The feet are white.

Nocturnal, it lives in burrows or cracks in the ground, lining its nest with soft vegetable debris. It eats insects, seeds and green vegetable matter, and digestion is aided by symbiotic micro-organisms. Litters of up to five are born in the nests at any time throughout the year. The young nipple-cling to their mothers as they move around. **(S194)**

GIANT RAT
(Reuse rot)
Cricetomys gambianus

Plate 26
No. 4

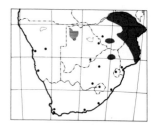

A huge rat; total length about 76 cm, tail about 42 cm.

Distribution is restricted to the northeastern and eastern parts of the Subregion, where it lives in evergreen forest or in woodland underbrush in the higher rainfall areas.

The body is grey to buffy grey in colour, the underparts whitish. There are distinct suffused dark patches around the eyes but the characteristic features are its large size and long tail, the terminal portion of which is white.

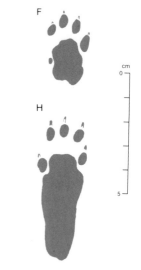

Predominantly nocturnal, the giant rat digs its own burrows, which are up to 2 m long with a chamber at the end floored with vegetable debris, the indigestible remains of food, stones and other detritus. It rests in these chambers during the day. It has cheek pouches in which smaller food items are collected to be carried back to the nest to be eaten. Larger food is eaten *in situ*. It is omnivorous, but predominantly vegetarian, subsisting on a diet of wild fruits, bulbs, tubers, seeds and, where available, orchard fruits such as mangoes and avocado pears, and agricultural products such as mealies, peanuts, peas and beans. It also eats insects. Litters of up to four young are born in the nests during the summer months.   **(S195)**

POUCHED MOUSE
(Wangsakmuis)
Saccostomus campestris

Plate 26
No. 2

Total length 16 cm, tail 4,5 cm

Widespread in the Subregion, except in the dry western areas and in parts of the southeast.

It has a robust body, large head and noticeably

Plate 26: 1. Pygmy rock mouse (p. 87).   **2.** Pouched mouse (p. 88).   **3.** White-tailed mouse (p. 87).   **4.** Giant rat (p. 88).

short tail, about a quarter of its total length. The body is grey or grey tinged with brown, the fur soft and silky, the underparts pure white. Those from the west are a lighter grey than those from the higher rainfall eastern sector. Like the giant rat, they have cheek pouches in which they collect food, to be transported back to the burrow where it can be eaten in safety.

The pouched mouse is predominantly a seed-eater, preferring the seeds of forbs and shrubs to grass seed, which forms only a small proportion of the food eaten. Litters of up to ten young are born in the burrows during the summer months. **(S196)**

LARGE-EARED MOUSE
(Bakoormuis)
Malacothrix typica

Plate 27
No. 4

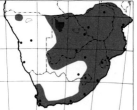

Total length about 11 cm, tail 3,6 cm
Occurs in the drier western parts of the Subregion, usually on hard ground with a short grass cover.

Colour varies geographically from pale reddish brown to buffy, but this species can be clearly identified by the characteristic dark pattern on the head and back and its large ears.

Nocturnal, it excavates deep burrows, 20 to 25 mm in diameter, with resting chambers, and lives on grass seed and green vegetable matter. Litters of up to six young are born in the burrows during the summer months. **(S197)**

GREY CLIMBING MOUSE
(Grysklimmuis)
Dendromus melanotis

Plate 27
No. 3

A small species; total length: males 15,6 cm, females 14,8 cm; tail: males 9 cm, females 8,8 cm.

Widespread in the southern coastal, eastern and northeastern parts of the Subregion, with isolated records from northern Namibia.

The body is ashy grey in colour with a diffused dark band down the mid-back and a dark spot on the forehead. This mouse is recognisable by its

---

Plate 27: 1. Brants' climbing mouse (p. 92). **2.** Chestnut climbing mouse, male and female (p. 92). **3.** Grey climbing mouse (p. 90). **4.** Large-eared mouse (p. 90). **5.** Fat mouse (p. 93).

small size, its colour and markings. Its tail is noticeably long and is semi-prehensile, it curls it around grass stems to steady itself when foraging.

It lives on grass seeds, with insects and particularly moths also figuring highly in the diet. Litters of up to four young are born in small ball-shaped nests in tall grass or bushes or in disused weaver or bishop bird nests. **(S199)**

The closely allied **Nyika climbing mouse (S198)** occurs only in the north-eastern parts of the Subregion and is rarely seen. It is slightly larger and redder or browner in colour.

BRANTS' CLIMBING MOUSE   Plate 27
(Brants se klimmuis)   No. 1
Dendromus mesomelas

The largest of the climbing mice; total length 17,5 cm, tail 10 cm.

An uncommon species, with a discontinuous distribution in the Subregion, where it is associated with tall grass or rank vegetation near water.

Dark reddish brown in colour, with a diffused black band down the mid-back, whitish underparts and a long semi-prehensile tail over half the total length.

Nocturnal and to some extent arboreal, it lives on grass seed and insects. Litters of up to four young are born in ball-shaped grass nests during the summer months.   **(S200)**

CHESTNUT CLIMBING MOUSE   Plate 27
(Roeskleurklimmuis)   No. 2
Dendromus mystacalis

Total length: males 15 cm, females 14 cm; tail: males 8,6 cm, females 8 cm.

Widespread in the northeastern parts of the Subregion, with isolated records from the south.

The body is bright chestnut, with a diffused black band down the mid-back. The underparts are pure white. The tail is long, semi-prehensile, and over half of the total length.

Nocturnal and to some extent arboreal, it lives on grass seeds and insects. Litters of up to four young are born in small ball-shaped grass nests in tall grass or bushes during the summer months. During the winter it will use holes in the ground.   **(S201)**

FAT MOUSE
(Vetmuis)
Steatomys pratensis

Plate 27
No. 5

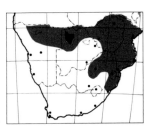

Total length 13 cm, tail 4,3 cm

Occurs in the northern and northeastern parts of the Subregion and is associated with the fringes of streams, rivers and swamps, where there is a sandy substrate.

Colour varies from lighter to darker shades of rusty brown; the flanks usually browner, the underparts and feet white. Characteristic features are the noticeably short tail, which is less than a third of total length; the fine sheen on its coat, and the pure white underparts.

It feeds on grass seeds and insects, including termites. Litters of up to nine young are born in grass-lined nests at the base of grass tussocks during the summer months. **(S202)**

Two other species of fat mouse occur, but are less common and have scattered and discontinuous distributions: the **tiny fat mouse (S203)** and **Kreb's fat mouse (S204)**, the former small with a white tail, the latter slightly larger than the fat mouse, and with a greyer body.

Order CARNIVORA. This Order was named at a time when it was thought that all its members were flesh-eaters, the name being derived from the Latin *carno,* flesh, and *voro,* to eat. We know now that not all of them eat flesh; in fact some, such as the African civet, are largely vegetarians. All are, however, fundamentally predators, and the Order includes species of very different shapes and sizes. Some, like the lion, are adapted to dealing with prey up to the size of the buffalo, others, like some of the mongooses, live predominantly on insects. In southern Africa the Order is represented by six Families and comprises 37 species, including one introduced species, the domestic cat, which is now feral in many parts of the area.

Family **HYAENIDAE.** Represented in the Subregion by two species, the brown hyaena and the spotted hyaena. Both species have four toes on the feet and immensely powerful jaws and teeth with which they can slice the toughest food and crack heavy bones. They have well developed anal glands and distinctive behaviours for depositing their secretions as scent marks on grass stems.

BROWN HYAENA
(Strandjut)

Hyaena brunnea

Plate 28
No. 2

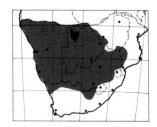

F

Shoulder height 80 cm; mean mass: males 40 kg, females 38,4 kg.

Resident in parts of the western, northern and northeastern sectors of the Subregion, but individuals wander widely at times and there are scattered records outside these sectors. The brown hyaena occurs predominantly in arid country, even utilising the western coastal desert.

The colour of the body, which is covered with long, coarse hair, varies from brown to nearly black with an off-white or tawny-white mantle covering the sides of the head and shoulders. The muzzle and face are naked and black. The limbs have dark transverse bands, the underparts are tawny or dirty white and the bushy tail dark brown or black. The upstanding ears rise to high, pointed tips.

The brown hyaena is nocturnal, foraging singly, but is associated in groups of males and females with fixed territories. The number in a group depends on food availability. Solitary nomadic males are also a feature of the social organisation, and these males are the ones primarily responsible for breeding. It lies up in holes or thick cover during the day. Predominantly a scavenger, it will take mammals, birds, reptiles, wild fruits and insects, but is a poor hunter, few capture attempts being successful.

Litters of up to four young are born in holes in the ground at any time of the year. Two or more females may have their litters in the same hole. All the members of the group carry food back to the den for the cubs. Unlike the spotted hyaena, it has no whooping call but, under stress, will yell, growl and grunt, and whine and squeal in greeting. **(S245)**

 ## SPOTTED HYAENA
(Gevlekte hiëna)

Crocuta crocuta

Plate 28
No. 3

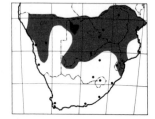

Shoulder height about 80 cm; mean mass: males 58 kg, females 70 kg.

Widespread in the northern parts of the Subregion in open country or open woodland. Its presence is dependent on adequate populations of medium-sized and large ungulates, its main food, in the absence of which it will turn to domestic stock, which has led to its eradication in many areas.

Massively built, with heavy forequarters and relatively lighter hindquarters, giving the impression of a sloping back. The background colour of the body is off-white or greyish white, tinged yellow, and the body has dark brown or blackish suffused spots, which tend to disappear with age. The head, neck and lower parts of the limbs are unspotted. The head is broad and massive, with a dark brown or nearly black muzzle and broad rounded ears. The body is covered with short, coarse hair and there is a crest of hair on the mid-back from the head to the shoulders, and a bushy black or dark brown tail.

The spotted hyaena lives in matriarchal clans, which occupy demarcated territories, but may forage alone or in groups, killing medium-sized or large mammals or scavenging. Litters of one or two young are born in holes in the ground at any time of the year. Clan females den together but each suckles only her own cubs. Clan members do not carry food to the cubs. The call is a series of long drawn-out *who-o-oops*, rising in pitch and sometimes trailing out in a low moaning. It also grunts, groans and giggles, and yells and whines particularly when squabbling at kills. **(S246)**

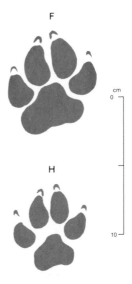

Family PROTELIDAE. This family contains a single species, the aardwolf, which somewhat resembles a diminutive hyaena. It has five toes on its front feet and a well developed anal gland that it uses for scent marking. Its cheekteeth are small and peg-like and are not used for chewing.

AARDWOLF
(Aardwolf)
Proteles cristatus

Plate 28
No. 1

Shoulder height about 50 cm, mean mass 8,8 kg.

Widespread throughout the Subregion, except in desert and forest. It has a wide habitat tolerance, with a tendency to prefer open country, but its occurrence depends on the availability of harvester termites.

The background colour of the body is pale buff to yellowish white, with four or five diffused black transverse stripes on the back and flanks; black muzzle, black transverse stripes on the upper parts of the limbs, neck and thighs, and black feet. A mane of long black and white hair extends down the neck and back to the bushy black-tipped tail. The mane is erected under stress and in territorial disputes. While the cheekteeth are peg-like and poorly developed, it has formidable canine teeth which are used in defence.

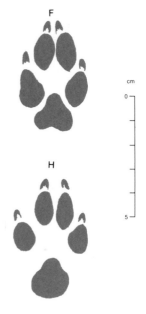

The aardwolf is territorial and lives in monogamous pairs. It forages alone at night and rests in holes in the ground which it adjusts to its requirements. It feeds almost exclusively on harvester termites which it licks off the soil surface; its teeth are ill-adapted to tougher food. Litters of up to four young are born in holes in the ground. Gestation is 90 days, births are usually during the summer. Under stress it growls loudly or gives an explosive bark, and under extreme stress roars surprisingly loudly for such a small species. **(S244)**

Family FELIDAE. Represented in the subregion by three genera and seven species: cheetah, leopard, lion, caracal, wild cat, small-spotted cat and serval; a well-defined and homogeneous assemblage. They are adept stalkers and killers, with teeth adapted to delivering the killing bite and to slicing the food into chunks convenient to swallow. In most species the curved claws are protected in sheaths when not in use. All have five digits on the front feet, four on the hind.

Plate 28: **1.** Aardwolf (p. 96). **2.** Brown hyaena (p. 94). **3.** Spotted hyaena (p. 94).

28

CHEETAH
(Jagluiperd)
Acinonyx jubatus

Plate 29
No. 1

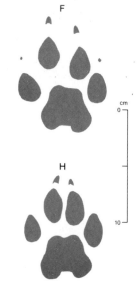

Shoulder height about 80 cm; mean mass: males 53,9 kg, females 43 kg.

The cheetah is confined to the northern and northeastern parts of the Subregion. It is generally associated with open country, but also occurs in open woodland.

The background colour of the body is buffy white, usually darker along the back, and is profusely covered with round or oval black spots. The spotting extends onto the proximal parts of the tail, which is about a third of the total length, the distal end with several black rings and a white tip. There is a distinct black band running from the forehead through the inside edges of the eyes to the corners of the mouth. The head is small and rounded and there is a mane of long hair from the nape of the neck to the top of the shoulders. The legs are long and spotted like the body, the underparts of the body white. The claws can be protracted but do not retract into sheaths as in other felids.

Diurnal; females solitary or with dependent young, males solitary or in groups of two or three. Their usual food is medium-sized to small bovids or the young of the larger. They are accounted the fastest mammals over short distances. Litters numbering up to five, more usually three, are born in the shelter of underbrush or tall grass at any time of the year. They chirrup when excited and have a bird-like contact call that carries long distances. **(S247)**

Plate 29:   1. Cheetah (p. 98).   **2.** Lion (p. 100).   **3.** Leopard (p. 100).

29

1

2

3

LEOPARD
(Luiperd)
Panthera pardus

Plate 29
No. 3

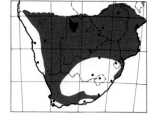

Shoulder height about 60 cm, but size varies throughout the range, individuals from the southwestern parts of the Subregion being smaller than those from the northeast. Mean mass: males from the southwestern Cape Province 36 kg, females 19 kg; males from Zimbabwe 60 kg, females 32 kg.

Widespread in the Subregion except in the central sector and in desert, and usually associated with broken country or forests.

The background colour is whitish to golden yellow with black spots on the limbs, head, flanks and hindquarters and rosettes on the remainder of the body. The underparts, including the under surface of the tail, are white with black spots. The ears are rounded and small, the tail slightly less than half the total length.

Nocturnal and solitary, leopards are secretive and cunning and are rarely seen except in conservation areas where they are habituated to vehicles. They take any warm-blooded prey, from mice to mammals twice their own mass. Their diet varies depending on the availability of prey species and in parts they can become problem animals where there is free-ranging domestic stock. Kills are often hoisted into trees where they are safe from scavengers. Litters of up to three young are born at any time throughout the year in sheltered places. Their most characteristic call is a rasping cough, but they also growl and purr. **(S248)**

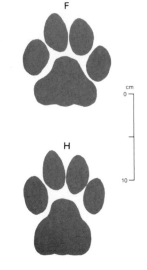

F

H

cm
0

10

LION
(Leeu)
Panthera leo

Plate 29
No. 2

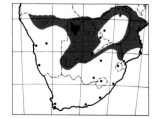

The largest of African carnivores; shoulder height: males 1,25 m, females 90 cm; mass: males up to 240 kg, females about 150 kg.

At one time, lions occurred throughout the

Subregion, but they are now found only in the northern and northeastern parts of the Subregion and in reserves in Natal.

Colour is pale sandy or tawny with white underparts, some individuals retaining traces of the spotting characteristic of the young on their limbs and underparts. The backs of the rounded ears are black and there is a tuft of long dark hair on the tip of the long tail. The males usually have a heavy mane of long hair on the head, neck and shoulders, which may be black. Maneless males are also found.

Lions live in prides of 2–10 females with their cubs and 1–4 attendant adult males. The prides have well-defined home ranges. The males tend to move between prides and often have to fight other males for possession of them. Lions are nocturnally active, spending the day resting in the shade. They feed on warm-blooded prey from mice to buffalo, but will take birds, reptiles and even insects. Occasionally they will tackle even larger prey and have been known to kill young elephants and hippopotamus. Success with large prey depends on their hunting in groups; the females do most of the hunting but at kills the males take precedence over other members of the pride. The females leave the prides to give birth to litters of up to six young at any time of the year. Cub mortality is high in early life. The roar of lions at night is a characteristic sound of the African night and may become communal, pride answering pride. They also grunt, growl and cough. **(S249)**

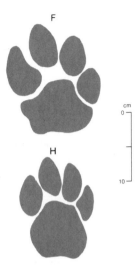

CARACAL
(Rooikat)
Felis caracal

Plate 30
No. 1

Shoulder height 40–45 cm; mass: males up to 22 kg, females 11,5 kg.

Widespread throughout the Subregion in open scrub and woodland.

The body colour varies from a silvery grey in the sourthern parts of the range to a pinkish red in the drier western areas, but may be sandy brown or brick red in the eastern higher rainfall areas. The underparts are pure white with

101

some indistinct spotting on the chest. The characteristic feature of the caracal is the high upstanding black-backed ears with tassels of long hair on the tips. It has a short, dark-tipped tail, slightly less than a third of total length, and robust limbs.

Nocturnal, solitary and secretive, the caracal is very quick in its actions and can catch live birds in the air when these are flushed at close quarters. It feeds predominantly on warm-blooded prey, which consists of mammals up to the size of impala and ground-living birds, and can become a problem animal where there is free-ranging small stock. Litters of up to four young are born in the shelter of thick bushes or rock crevices, usually during the summer. The young vocalise with a bird-like twittering, the adults with a soft, guttural *meeuw*. **(S250)**

F

H

cm

0

5

AFRICAN WILD CAT
(Vaalboskat)
Felis lybica

Plate 30
No. 3

Shoulder height about 35 cm; mean mass: males 5,1 kg, females 4,2 kg.

Widespread throughout the Subregion except in desert.

In the drier western parts of the Subregion colour is light sandy with an indistinct pattern of transverse reddish brown bands on the back and limbs and a black-tipped tail. In the eastern parts it is much greyer, the bands darker and more distinct. It is longer in the legs than the domestic cat and the backs of the ears are reddish. The underparts may be whitish or tinged reddish, with indistinct dark or reddish spots. It crosses freely with domestic cats, the progeny being shorter in the legs and losing totally, or to varying extents, the reddish colour on the back of the ears.

Plate 30: **1.** Caracal (p. 101). **2.** Small-spotted cat (p. 104). **3.** African wild cat (p. 102). **4.** Serval (p. 105).

30

1

2

3

4

The wild cat is nocturnal and usually solitary, but pairs may hunt together. It lives predominantly on mice but will take birds, reptiles, insects and other invertebrates. The largest prey recorded are scrub hares and young canerats. Litters of up to five are born in dense underbrush or other substantial cover, usually during the summer months. It *meeuws* like a domestic cat.

(S251)

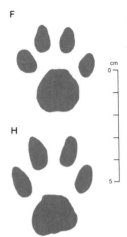

The **domestic cat (S254)** is feral in many parts of the African mainland as well as on Marion Island in the Subantarctic.

SMALL-SPOTTED CAT
(Klein gekolde kat)
Felis nigripes

Plate 30
No. 2

The smallest of our cats; shoulder height about 20–25 cm; mean mass: males 1,6 kg, females 1,1 kg.

Occurs only in the drier central parts of the Subregion and is associated with dry, open scrub country.

The background colour in the south is cinnamon buff, further north tawny to off-white, with dark or rusty-tinged bands on the top of the shoulders and upper parts of the limbs; the remainder of the body has similarly coloured spots. The underparts are white in the northern populations, buffy in the southern. There are two or three throat rings, which in the southern populations are black, in the northern rufous. The tail is short and black-tipped, slightly less than a third of total length. The back of the ears is the same colour as the background colour of the body, never reddish as in the wild cat. The small-spotted cat was formerly known as the black-footed cat, but this name is inappropriate as the African wild cat also has black hair under the feet.

It is nocturnal, solitary and secretive, living predominantly on mice, insects and other invertebrates, reptiles and small birds. Litters of up to three are born during the summer months.

(S252)

SERVAL
(Tierboskat)
Felis serval

Plate 30
No. 4

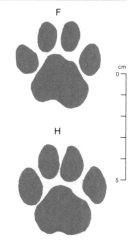

F

H

cm
0

5

Shoulder height 60 cm; mean mass: males 11 kg, females 9,7 kg.

Occurs only in the better-watered northern, northeastern and southeastern parts of the Subregion. Proximity to water appears to be an essential habitat requirement, together with the availability of cover in the form of stands of tall grass or underbrush.

The serval is an elegant species, with its long legs and neck, small head and high upstanding ears. The background colour of the body may vary from white to light golden yellow, with a pattern of black bands and spots. The short tail, which is less than a third of total length, is ringed with black and has a black tip. The upper parts of the front legs are banded with black.

Nocturnal, occurring singly or in pairs, it locates its prey by sight or hearing, killing it either by slapping it with a front foot or by pouncing on it with both feet, like a dog. It lives principally on rodents, especially vlei rats and multimammate mice, but will take birds, reptiles and insects. Litters of up to three young are born in stands of tall grass or underbrush during the summer months. Vocalisations include a high-pitched wail and a plaintive *meeuw* and it will also growl and spit. **(S253)**

Family CANIDAE. This Family is represented in the Subregion by three subfamilies: OTOCYONINAE, the bat-eared fox; CANINAE, the black-backed and side-striped jackals and the Cape fox, and SIMOCYONINAE, the wild dog. All are long-legged carnivores.

BAT-EARED FOX
(Bakoorvos)
Otocyon megalotis

Plate 31
No. 2

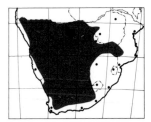

Shoulder height about 30 cm; mean mass: males 4 kg, females 4,1 kg.

Occurs in the drier western parts of the Subregion and is particularly associated with open country.

105

Distinctive features are the thick coat of long, grey or buffy grey hair, the black muzzle, the white band across the forehead, the black legs and the huge rounded ears. The lower parts of the limbs and tip of the bushy tail are black. There are five digits on the front feet, armed with long claws for digging, the first not marking in the spoor, and four on the hind.

The bat-eared fox is both nocturnal and diurnal and occurs singly or more commonly in pairs. It is predominantly insectivorous but will take other invertebrates, mice, reptiles and small birds. It lives in holes in the ground, where litters of up to six young are born in the summer; only four are usually reared. The call is a soft *who-who* and, under stress, it growls and vocalises with a loud metallic chattering. **(S255)**

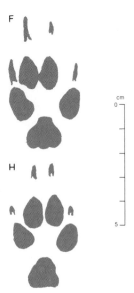

BLACK-BACKED JACKAL
(Rooijakkals)
Canis mesomelas

Plate 31
No. 3

Shoulder height 38 cm; mean mass: males 7,9 kg, females 6,6 kg.

Widespread throughout the Subregion, even in arid areas, being replaced in the better-watered northern and northeastern parts by the side-striped jackal.

Plate 31: 1. Cape fox (p. 109). **2.** Bat-eared fox (p. 105). **3.** Black-backed jackal (p. 106). **4.** Side-striped jackal (p. 108). **5.** Wild dog (p. 109).

31

Characteristic features are the dark saddle on the back, which extends from the nape of the neck to the tail, the reddish flanks and limbs of the adults, and the black-tipped bushy tail.

Nocturnal and diurnal, and usually solitary, it is wary and cunning. Adults live in territorial pairs. It may be encountered singly or in pairs or families. Large numbers gather at rich food sources. It eats many insects and will take carrion and warm-blooded prey up to the size of an impala. It is regarded as a problem animal by some small stock farmers. As it also eats fish, reptiles, wild fruits, peanuts and green mealies it is considered to be omnivorous. Litters of up to six young are born in holes in the ground during the late winter or early summer months. The call is a long drawn-out *nyaaa* followed by a stacatto *ya-ya-ya-ya* and is one of the familiar sounds of the African night. **(S259)**

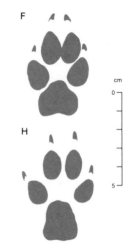

SIDE-STRIPED JACKAL

Plate 31
No. 4

(Witkwasjakkals)
Canis adustus

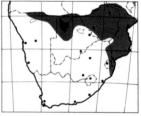

Shoulder height 38 cm; mean mass: males 9,4 kg, females 8,3 kg.

Occurs in the northern and northeastern parts of the Subregion in well-watered habitat, favouring areas of thickly wooded country; locally common, otherwise rare.

Greyish or greyish buff in colour with a suffused light lateral stripe on the flanks and a similar stripe arising from this across the back just behind the shoulders. The tail is black and bushy, with a characteristic white tip. The back and upper parts of the limbs are tinged reddish, the lower parts of the hind legs plain buffy white. There are five digits on the front feet, four on the hind, armed with claws. The first digits of the front feet do not mark in the spoor.

Nocturnal and solitary, the side-striped jackal is omnivorous, living on wild fruits, small mammals, carrion, insects and small birds. Where available, peanuts, green mealies, the seeds of

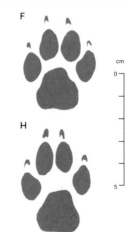

agricultural crops, and orchard fruits and pumpkins are taken. Litters of up to six young are born in holes in the ground in spring or summer. The call is a series of melancholy yaps, without the long drawn-out call of the black-backed jackal. **(S258)**

CAPE FOX   Plate 31
(Silwervos)   No. 1
Vulpes chama

Shoulder height 35 cm; mean mass: males 3 kg, females 2,9 kg.
   Widespread in the drier western parts of the Subregion in open country.
   A small, dainty fox, its characteristic features are its dark thick bushy tail, the silvery coloured upper parts of the body, the reddish tinged head and limbs, and the face with its profuse sprinkling of white hair. There are five digits on the front feet, four on the hind. The first digits of the front feet do not mark in the spoor.
   Nocturnal and usually solitary, it lies up in holes in the ground or in the cover of underbrush. It feeds on insects, mice, small mammals and inverte-brates, and will take wild fruits, reptiles, small birds and their eggs. Litters of up to five young are born in holes during the early summer months. The call is a high-pitched howl and a bark, the latter in alarm. **(S257)**

WILD DOG   Plate 31
(Wildehond)   No. 5
Lycaon pictus

Shoulder height 75 cm, mass 26–28 kg.
   Found in the northern and northeastern parts of the Subregion where there are adequate populations of bovids, which are its principal food. In the absence of these, it will turn to domestic stock, which has led to its extermination as vermin in many parts of its formerly wide range. It is now Africa's most endangered large carnivore.

The wild dog is unmistakable, with its long legs, large rounded ears and blotched black, yellow and white coat.

It is diurnal, living and hunting in packs of usually 8–12. They will tackle prey up to the size of wildebeest, but more usually they take medium-sized bovids such as impala or springbok by running them down. When excited they vocalise with a bird-like twittering, but will yelp, bark or growl and locate each other with a musical *hooo-hooo* call. Usually only the dominant female in the pack breeds, producing a litter of up to 21, usually about 12 puppies, in a hole in the ground. Most pups are born in mid-winter. The mother and other members of the pack regurgitate food for the young and all are involved in their wellbeing and defence. **(S256)**

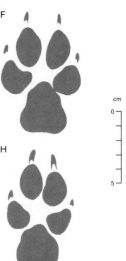

F

H

cm

0

5

Family **MUSTELIDAE.** This Family is represented in the Subregion by five species, two aquatic and three terrestrial, grouped into three Subfamilies: the LUTRINAE, the clawless and spotted-necked otters; the MUSTELINAE, the striped polecat and striped weasel and the MELLIVORINAE, the honey badger. Members have anal glands whose secretion is strong smelling and is used in defence.

CAPE CLAWLESS OTTER Plate 32
(Groot otter) No. 4
Aonyx capensis

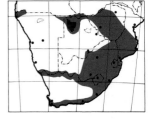

The larger of the two otters in the Subregion; total length about 1,25 m; mean mass: males 12,3 kg, females 14,3 kg.

An aquatic species, living in fresh or sea water

Plate 32: **1.** Striped polecat (p. 113). **2.** Striped weasel (p. 113). **3.** Spotted-necked otter (p. 112). **4.** Cape clawless otter (p. 110).

and widespread in the Subregion where there is suitable habitat.

Colour varies from light to very dark brown, the underparts usually lighter than the upper. The hair on the forehead, top of the head and shoulders has a silvery sheen. A characteristic feature is the white chin, throat, upper chest and sides of the neck. A thick guard coat overlies dense underfur, the head is broad and rounded and the broad, tapering tail is flattened ventrally to act as a rudder. There are five digits on the feet, those on the hind feet webbed for propulsion when swimming, and with rudimentary nails. The nasal apertures are set in slits, which can be closed at will when diving.

The Cape clawless otter is both nocturnal and diurnal and occurs solitarily or in pairs. It deposits its scats, which usually contain pieces of crab shells, in latrines. In freshwater habitats it eats mainly crabs and frogs and a few insects, reptiles, molluscs and birds. In the sea it lives on fish, crustaceans and octopus. Litters of two young are born in holes in the banks of rivers and dams or along the sea coast at any time of the year. The females have two pairs of abdominal mammae. **(S260)**

SPOTTED-NECKED OTTER

(Klein otter)

Lutra maculicollis

Plate 32
No. 3

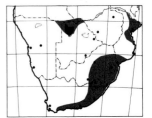

Total length about 1 m; mass: males about 4,5 kg, females 3,5 kg.

Occurs only in the south and southeast and in parts of the north and northeast of the Subregion. It is more closely confined to an aquatic habitat than the clawless otter and is less at home on dry land.

Colour varies from chocolate brown to reddish brown, the throat and upper chest mottled with creamy white, the underparts the same colour as the upper. It is slimmer in build than the clawless otter. The long tapering tail is flattened underneath to assist in swimming and the five webbed digits on the feet are equipped with creamy white claws.

Active in the early morning and late afternoon when it forages for fish, which is its principal food, but it will also take crabs, molluscs and frogs and occasionally insects and small birds. Litters of up to two young are born in holes or in secluded areas in reed beds during the summer months. The females have two pairs of abdominal mammae. **(S261)**

STRIPED WEASEL

(Slangmuishond)
Poecilogale albinucha

Plate 32
No. 2

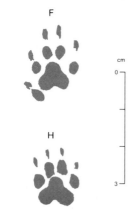

F

H

Total length 45 cm, tail 16 cm; mean mass: males 260 g, females 180 g.

So few records of this species are available that it is impossible to clearly define its distribution. Apart from the southeastern parts of the Subregion and along the south coast only scattered records exist.

It has very short legs and a low-slung, elongated body, which is jet black with four longitudinal white or yellowish white bands down the back; the forehead and top of the head are white, the fur short and closely adpressed to the body. The white tail is about a third of the total length.

The striped weasel is usually solitary, with both nocturnal and diurnal activity. It lives on mice and possibly molerats, which its small size and sinuous body allow it to hunt and capture in their burrows. It is an avid digger and constructs its own burrows with a chamber in which litters of up to three young are born during the summer months. The females have a pair of abdominal and one or two pairs of inguinal mammae. **(S263)**

STRIPED POLECAT

(Stinkmuishond)
Ictonyx striatus

Plate 32
No. 1

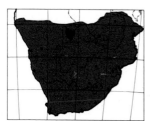

Total length 62 cm, tail 26 cm; mean mass: males 970 g, females 713 g.

Widespread throughout the Subregion.

The body is jet black with white patches on

the forehead and cheeks, four longitudinal bands down the back, and a predominantly white tail. The pattern of markings is similar to that of the striped weasel, from which the striped polecat can be distinguished by the longer hair on the body, the bushy tail, longer legs, less sinuous body and more pointed snout.

F

H

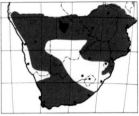

The polecat is well known for the evil-smelling and highly persistent secretion from the anal glands that it uses in self-defence. It is nocturnal and solitary, living in holes in the ground. It is predominantly insectivorous. Litters of up to three young are born during the summer months in holes. The females have a pair of abdominal and a pair of inguinal mammae. **(S264)**

HONEY BADGER
(Ratel)
Mellivora capensis

Plate 33
No. 3

Total length about 95 cm, tail 22 cm, mass about 12 kg.

Widespread but sparsely distributed throughout the Subregion, except in desert.

Jet black in colour, with a broad white or greyish white saddle from just above the eyes to the tail, which is about a quarter of the total length. The limbs are short and stocky, the five digits on the front feet armed with long, powerfully built, knife-like claws, those on the five hind digits broad and hollowed out underneath.

Nocturnal and generally solitary, but often found in pairs. The honey badger is aggressive and fearless and if annoyed has been known to put up a spirited defence, even against lions. It walks with a rolling gait, sniffing around for food which consists of scorpions, mice, baboon spiders, birds, reptiles, bee larvae and honey. Litters of two young are born during the summer months. The females have two pairs of abdominal mammae. **(S262)**

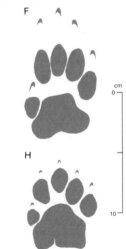

Family **VIVERRIDAE**. This large and heterogeneous Family is represented in the Subregion by 16 species grouped in three Subfamilies: the VIVERRINAE, the civet and two genets; the HERPESTINAE, 11 species of mongoose and the suricate, and the NANDINIINAE, the tree civet. The principal characters of the various Subfamilies are reflected in the teeth, which may be adapted to slicing, breaking or crushing the food, and in other morphological features. The tree civet is unique among the carnivores in that the bullae of the ears are un-ossified.

SMALL-SPOTTED GENET
(Kleinkolmuskejaatkat)
Genetta genetta

Plate 33
No. 1

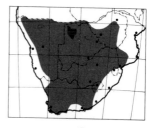

Total length about 95 cm, tail 46 cm, mean mass: males 1,8 kg, females 1,9 kg.

Widespread throughout the central and western parts of the Subregion in open scrub and woodland. It is replaced in the east by the large-spotted genet, the two species occurring together in parts of the intermediate range.

The colour of the body is white or buffy white, with small black or rusty coloured spots. The tops of the shoulders have black bars and the tail, which is about half the total length, is ringed with black and has a white tip. The lower parts of the hind limbs are usually black. Small-spotted genets have distinctive black and white facial markings, high upstanding, rounded ears and a distinct erectile crest of long black hair down the mid-back.

Nocturnal and usually solitary, it is a proficient climber, taking to the trees when disturbed. It rests in holes or other sheltered places during the day. When walking, the tail is held out horizontally behind it. It lives on insects, mice and small birds, but will take spiders, scorpions, hunting spiders, reptiles and wild fruits. Litters of up to four young are born in holes in the ground or hollow trees during the summer months. The females have two pairs of abdominal mammae. **(S267)**

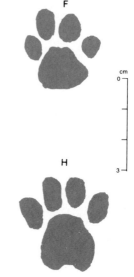

F

cm
0

H

3

LARGE-SPOTTED GENET
(Rooikolmuskejaatkat)
Genetta tigrina

Plate 33
No. 2

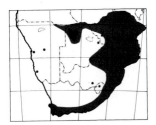

Total length 95 cm; tail 46 cm; mean mass: males 1,8 kg, females 1,7 kg.

Unlike the small-spotted genet, this species avoids arid country and occurs in the northern, eastern and southern better-watered parts of the Subregion. In parts, however, the two species occur together.

The background colour of the body varies from off-white to buffy white with a pattern of black or rusty coloured spots and blotches, these usually larger than in the small-spotted genet, and with similarly coloured bands on the shoulders. The tail is banded with black or rusty and has a black tip. The limbs are off-white or buffy white. The face has distinctive dark brown and white markings. The hair is softer than that of the small-spotted genet and the dorsal crest may or may not be present but, at most, is confined to the lower mid-back.

Nocturnal and usually solitary, its habits and food are similar to those of the small-spotted genet. Litters of up to five young are born in holes or other sheltered places during the summer months. The females have two pairs of abdominal mammae. **(S268)**

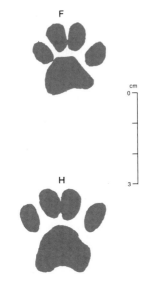

F

H

cm
0

3

TREE CIVET
(Boomsiwet)
Nandinia binotata

Plate 34
No. 1

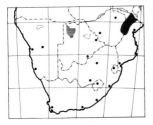

Total length about 95 cm, tail 46 cm, mean mass about 2 kg.

Closely confined to forested areas in the extreme northeastern parts of the Subregion.

Plate 33: 1. Small-spotted genet (p. 115). **2.** Large-spotted genet (p. 116). **3.** Honey badger (p. 114).

33

The coat appears brown in the field, but is covered with irregularly shaped indistinct dark brown spots on a brown background and, characteristically, has a white or yellowish spot above the shoulders on either side. The hair is long and soft; the tail, which is about half the total length, is bushy and shows some banding or spotting towards the base, but is otherwise buffy brown in colour. There are five digits on the feet, armed with sharp, curved protractile claws.

Nocturnal, solitary and predominantly arboreal, it climbs or leaps among the branches of tall trees, the tail, curved upwards, acting as a balancing organ. During the day it rests in hollow trees or among dense foliage. It is slower in its movements than the genets and is prone to sit tight if caught in the beam of a dazzling light. Predominantly vegetarian, it lives on wild fruits, but will take birds, mice and termites and has been known to take bats. Little is known about its reproduction under Subregion conditions.

(S265)

F

H

cm
0
3

AFRICAN CIVET

(Afrikaanse siwet)
Civettictis civetta

Plate 34
No. 4

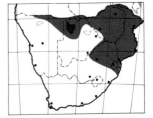

Total length about 1,3 m, tail 46 cm; mean mass: males 10,9 kg, females 11,6 kg.

Widely distributed in the northern and north-eastern parts of the Subregion, in forest and woodland where water is available.

Black in colour, with a conspicuous and very varied pattern of bands and blotches of white on the body, no two being exactly alike in markings. The

---

Plate 34: **1.** Tree civet (p. 116). **2.** Selous' mongoose (p. 121). **3.** Suricate (p. 120). **4.** African civet (p. 118).

118

long black bushy tail is about half the total length, with some white markings at the base. The lower parts of the limbs are black and there are five digits on the feet, armed with stout, curved claws. The first digits are set well back from the others and do not mark in the spoor. The hair is long and coarse and there is an erectile crest of long hair down the mid-back.

Nocturnal and solitary, when alarmed it tends to freeze and then either slink off or explode into action, bounding away to safety. Scats are deposited in latrines which, with prolonged use, are sometimes very large. It feeds on insects, wild fruits, mice, reptiles and birds and will take frogs, millipedes and other invertebrates. Litters of up to four young are born in holes or dense underbrush during the summer.   **(S266)**

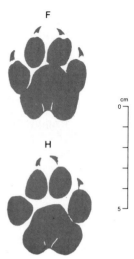

F

H

cm
0
5

SURICATE

(Stokstertmeerkat)
Suricata suricatta

Plate 34
No. 3

Total length about 50 cm, mean mass about 730 g, females sometimes as much as 950 g.

Widespread throughout the more arid parts of southern Africa.

Overall colour is silvery brown, individuals from the northwestern parts of the range paler than those from the southern. Characteristic features are the dark mottling on the back, extending from the shoulders to the tail, which may form transverse bands; the slender tapering, dark-tipped tail, and the dark rings around the eyes.

Diurnal, and highly social, it lives in warrens housing up to 30 individuals, sometimes sharing these with ground squirrels or yellow mongoose. It forages in groups and feeds predominantly on insects, particularly beetle larvae, but will take scorpions and lizards, centipedes and millipedes. Litters of about three young are born during the summer months and are raised by the whole group. The females have three pairs of abdominal mammae.   **(S269)**

SELOUS' MONGOOSE

Plate 34
No. 2

(Klein witstertmuishond)
Paracynictis selousi

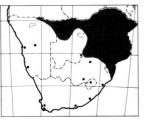

Total length about 78 cm, tail 38 cm, mean mass 1,8 kg.

Occurs only in the northeastern parts of the Subregion in open country, frequenting vleis, floodplain and grassland.

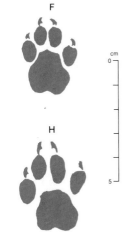

Colour is tawny or greyish, the lower parts of the limbs black. A characteristic feature is the broad white tip to the tail, never so extensive as in the white-tailed mongoose, which is much larger and darker in colour and has longer legs.

Nocturnal and usually solitary, it excavates its own burrows, which have a number of entrances. It walks quickly with its tail held out horizontally behind it and may rise on its back legs to survey the surrounding terrain. It is insectivorous but will take mice, reptiles, frogs and small birds. Litters of up to three young are born in the burrows during the summer months. The females have three pairs of abdominal mammae. **(S270)**

BUSHY-TAILED MONGOOSE

Plate 35
No. 1

(Borselstertmuishond)
Bdeogale crassicauda

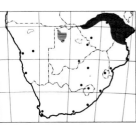

Total length about 70 cm, tail about 26 cm; mean mass: males 1,9 kg, females 1,6 kg.

Uncommon, occurring only in a restricted area in the northeastern parts of the Subregion. It is associated with rocky outcrops at low altitudes, often in the vicinity of rivers.

In the field it looks black, although the coat is usually grizzled with white flecking. The hair is long, especially on the bushy tail, where it is as long on the tip as at the base. There are four digits on the feet. The forefeet are armed with long, stout, curved claws, those on the hind feet are even longer, as they are not subject to the same wear in digging.

The bushy-tailed mongoose is active in the early morning and late evening as well as at night. It is a solitary species about which little is known. Insectivorous, it also eats reptiles, mice and scorpions, spiders and other invertebrates. Females have a pair of inguinal mammae. **(S271)**

YELLOW MONGOOSE
(Witkwasmuishond)
Cynictis penicillata

Plate 35
No. 3

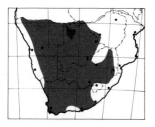

Total length varies geographically from 50 to 60 cm, tail about 22 cm; mass varies geographically: males 600–800 g, females 550–650 g.

Widespread in the drier parts of the Subregion in open scrub, grassland and karroid associations.

In the southern parts of its range the yellow mongoose is tawny yellow or reddish yellow in colour, in the north it is grey, with a gradual transition in colour from south to north. The tail is covered with long hair and in the yellower individuals has a distinct white tip, which is lacking in the greyer. There are five digits on the forefeet, four on the hind; the second to the fifth digits on the front feet are armed with long claws, those on the hind feet shorter. The first digit on the feet is set well back from the remainder and does not mark in the spoor. The upper lip is entire with no central groove.

Predominantly diurnal, it is a common feature of the wildlife seen in the Karoo and open areas of the Orange Free State during the day. It lives in colonies of up to 20 in warrens, but scatters to forage. It lives on insects, but will take other invertebrates, mice, and occasionally birds and carrion. Litters of up to five young are born in the warrens during the summer, with odd births at other times of the year. The whole group contributes to their upbringing. The females have three pairs of abdominal mammae.   **(S272)**

LARGE GREY MONGOOSE
(Groot grysmuishond)
Herpestes ichneumon

Plate 35
No. 5

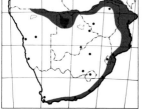

Total length about 1 m, tail about 52 cm, mean mass: males 3,4 kg, females 3,1 kg.

Occurs in the northern, eastern and extreme southern coastal parts of the Subregion, on the fringes of rivers, swamps, lakes and dams and in humid and sub-humid grassland in Natal.

Plate 35: 1. Bushy-tailed mongoose (p. 121). **2.** Small grey mongoose (p. 125). **3.** Yellow mongoose (p. 122). **4.** Slender mongoose (p. 124). **5.** Large grey mongoose (p. 122).

35

The large grey mongoose has an elongated body and head, with a pointed muzzle. The tail is about half the total length, with a broad black tip. Colour is dark grey, the lower parts of the relatively short limbs black, the hair long and coarse. There are five digits on the feet, each with swollen digital pads and long curved claws. The first digits are set well back from the others and do not mark in the spoor.

Diurnal with some nocturnal activity, it is solitary but has been seen in pairs or family parties. It rests in the shelter of riverine underbrush or reed beds. Under stress it erects the hair on the body and tail and vocalises with a loud *kie-kie-kie* or growls softly, or may freeze, lying flat on the ground. It lives on mice and birds, with frogs, reptiles and insects an important part of the diet. Litters of two are born in early summer. The females have three pairs of mammae.

(S273)

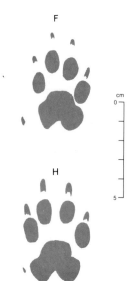

SLENDER MONGOOSE
(Swartkwasmuishond)
Galerella sanguinea

Plate 35
No. 4

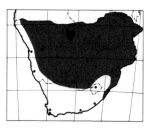

Total length about 60 cm, tail about 28 cm, mean mass: males 640 g, females 460 g.

Widespread in the Subregion except in the southern parts, where it is replaced by the small grey mongoose. Catholic in its habitat requirements and found wherever there is cover.

Colour varies from fiery red to grizzled grey; in Kaokoland and other parts of northern Namibia and occasionally elsewhere it is very dark reddish brown and appears black in the field. The slender mongoose is small and short-legged, with a sinuous body and a long black-tipped tail. There are five digits on the feet, the first set far back from the others and not generally marking in the spoor. Each digit is armed with a short, curved, sharp claw. The upper lip is divided by a central groove.

Diurnal and solitary, it tends to use tracks and

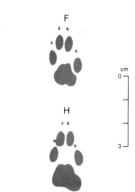

is often seen crossing roads, diving for cover with the tail cocked vertically. It rests in underbrush or holes in the ground, being small enough to use holes in termitaria. Predominantly insectivorous, it wil also take small reptiles, mice, birds, wild fruits and frogs. Litters of up to two young are born in holes during the summer. The females have one to three pairs of abdominal mammae. **(S274)**

Skull shape and coat colour suggest that there are two other species of slender mongoose: *Galerella nigrata,* bright reddish brown or dark brown from north and central Namibia, and *G. swalius,* greyish yellow with no reddish tinge from south and central Namibia.

SMALL GREY MONGOOSE
(Klein grysmuishond)
Galerella purverulenta

Plate 35
No. 2

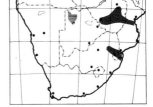

Total length about 65 cm, tail about 30 cm, mean mass: males 900 g, females 700 g.

Occurs only in the southern parts of the Subregion, where it replaces the slender mongoose.

Catholic in its habitat requirements, it occurs in open karroid areas as well as in forest.

In the field it appears dark grey, although the individual hairs are annulated with bands of black and white or buff, giving the coat a grizzled appearance. The tail, which is about half the total length, is the same colour as the body and may or may not have an indistinct dark tip. It never cocks its tail vertically as does the slender mongoose. There are five digits on the feet, the first digit set well back from the others and not marking in the spoor. Each digit is armed with a short, curved, sharp claw. The upper lip is grooved centrally.

Diurnal and solitary, it rests during the heat of the day in holes. Insects and mice are important in its diet; which predominates depends on locality. It will also take small birds, reptiles, small invertebrates and carrion from road kills. Litters of up to two are born in holes during the summer. **(S275)**

MELLER'S MONGOOSE
(Meller se muishond)
Rhynchogale melleri

Plate 36
No. 1

Total length about 80 cm, tail about 36 cm, mean mass: males 2,3 kg, females 3 kg.

Uncommon; distribution is limited to two areas in the northeast of the Subregion, where it occurs in open woodland or on grassland where there are termitaria.

Light brown or greyish brown in colour, the tail is slightly less than half of the total length, its basal portion the same colour as the body, the terminal half black, brown or white. When it is white this species may be confused with Selous' or the white-tailed mongoose, but the lower portion of the limbs in these two species is black, whereas in Meller's it is the same colour as the body, never black. (The white-tailed mongoose is also darker in colour and considerably larger, with longer legs.) There are five digits on each foot, of which four mark in the spoor, and the upper lip is not grooved centrally as in these other two species.

Nocturnal and generally solitary; its teeth are adapted to grinding soft food and it lives almost exclusively on termites, but will also eat other insects, small reptiles and frogs. Litters of up to three young are born in holes during the summer months. The females have two pairs of abdominal mammae. **(S276)**

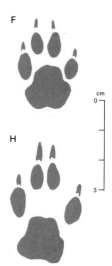

WHITE-TAILED MONGOOSE

Plate 36

No. 5

(Witstertmuishond)

Ichneumia albicauda

A large species; total length about 1,1 m, tail about 42 cm, mean mass: males 4,5 kg, females 4,1 kg.

Widespread in the better-watered northern, northeastern and eastern parts of the Subregion, in woodland or in riverine associations.

Dark greyish black in colour with relatively long jet black legs, its most conspicuous feature is the tail, which is slightly less than half the total length and white for four-fifths of its length towards the tip. It has the appearance of

Plate 36: **1.** Meller's mongoose (p. 125). **2.** Water mongoose (p. 128). **3.** Banded mongoose (p. 129). **4.** Dwarf mongoose (p. 130). **5.** White-tailed mongoose (p. 126).

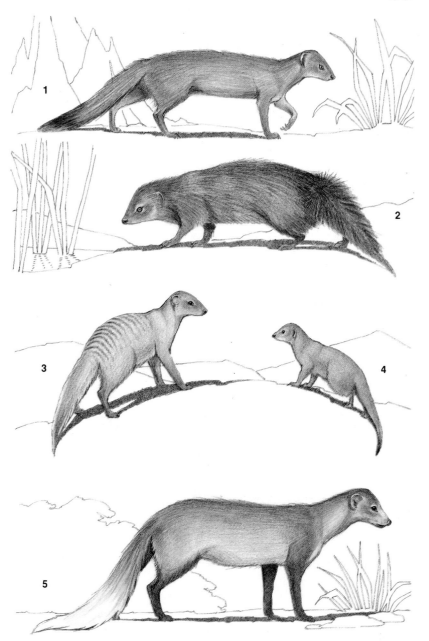

being heavier at the hindquarters than at the fore as the hair on the hindquarters is considerably longer. There are five digits on each foot and the upper lip is grooved centrally.

Nocturnal and generally solitary, although occasionally family parties forage together. It is an accomplished digger, though it may use antbear or springhare holes or crevices in rocky areas in which to rest during the day. Predominantly insectivorous, it will eat frogs, mice, reptiles, scorpions, sun spiders and wild fruits and grub for termites, beetles and beetle larvae in litter, under cowpats and in manure heaps. Litters of up to three young are born in holes during the summer months. The females have three pairs of abdominal mammae.   **(S277)**

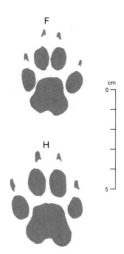

WATER MONGOOSE

Plate 36
No. 2

(Kommetjiegatmuishond)
Atilax paludinosus

Total length about 85 cm, tail about 36 cm, mean mass 3,4 kg.

Widespread, except in the drier central parts of the Subregion, in association with well-watered areas, especially along streams and rivers and on the fringes of swamps, dams, tidal estuaries and wet vleis.

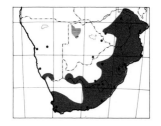

Colour varies greatly from reddish brown to black, the limbs darker in colour than the body. The hair is long and coarse, and that on the tail, which is slightly less than half the total length, is long at the base, tapering off towards the tip, and is usually a shade darker in colour than the body. There are five elongated digits on each foot, without the interdigital web that is present in all other viverrids. When walking on mud the digits tend to splay, which shows in the spoor. The head is broad, with a short muzzle, and the upper lip is grooved centrally.

Active from first light in the morning until the day warms up and then again towards evening, nesting deep in the shelter of riverine underbrush

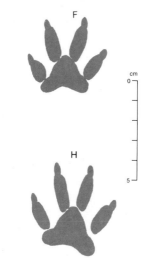

or reed beds during the heat of the day and at night. The water mongoose is solitary, although females may be accompanied by young. It feeds on frogs and crabs and will take mice, insects and fish. Crabs are forked out of holes in river banks with the long digits of the front feet and the carapace is usually discarded. Dry carapaces with other small portions found on river banks are a sign of the presence of water mongoose. Otters, which also eat crabs, usually break these up in eating. Little is known about its reproduction, although it appears that litters of one or two young are born during the summer months. The females have three pairs of abdominal mammae. **(S278)**

BANDED MONGOOSE   Plate 36
(Gebande muishond)   No. 3
Mungos mungo

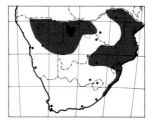

Total length about 54 cm, tail about 20 cm, mean mass: males 1,3 kg, females 1,4 kg.

Occurs in the northern and eastern parts of the Subregion in open woodland where there is detritus such as fallen logs and other debris.

The colour varies: individuals from the northern and northeastern areas are grizzled grey, those from Natal a much darker grizzled grey with a wash of reddish brown on the lower parts of the back, and black feet. The characteristic feature of the species is the series of up to about 15 transverse black bands from the midback to the base of the tail, which gives them their name. There are five digits on the feet; those on the front feet, with long curved claws, are adapted to scratching for food.

The banded mongoose is diurnal and lives in packs of up to about 30, resting at night in holes. It lives predominantly on insects and insect larvae but will take other invertebrates, mice and wild fruits. Litters of up to eight are born in grass-lined chambers in the refuges during the summer. The young are raised com-

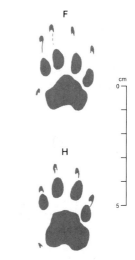

munally. The females have three pairs of abdominal mammae. Individuals in the packs maintain contact by twittering, the strident chittering of members warning the pack to slip off quietly to safety. **(S279)**

129

DWARF MONGOOSE
(Dwergmuishond)
Helogale parvula

Plate 36
No. 4

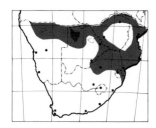

A small species: total length about 38 cm, tail about 17 cm, mean mass 268 g.

Widespread in the northern, northeastern and eastern parts of the Subregion in dry open woodland and on grassland where there is substrate litter and termitaria.

Colour appears black or very dark brown in the field, although the dark coat is grizzled with white or buff. There are five digits on the feet, the claws on the forefeet long, curved and adapted to scratching and digging. The upper lip is grooved centrally.

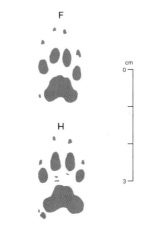

The dwarf mongoose is diurnal and lives in packs of up to 30, which use permanent holes, usually in termitaria and marked by an accumulation of scats near the entrances, with many known refuges scattered throughout the home range. It burrows deeply. When foraging, contact between members is maintained by vocalising in abrupt *perrips* or musical *chucks*. The alarm call is a sharp *chuchwee,* the pack freezing and then quietly scuttling off to cover. It lives mostly on insects and insect larvae but will take other invertebrates, reptiles and small mice. In the smaller packs only the dominant females breed, producing litters of up to four young during the summer. They are raised by the whole group. The females have three pairs of abdominal mammae. **(S280)**

Order **TUBULIDENTATA**, Family **ORYCTEROPODIDAE**. The antbear, often known as the aardvark, is the only member of this Order. It has no incisor or canine teeth, the cheekteeth consisting of a row of five rootless, rounded, flat-faced teeth without enamel in each half of the jaws. It hardly requires teeth as mastication of the food is provided for in a muscular pyloric area in the stomach, which functions like a gizzard, grinding up the food, mixed as it is with sand and soil. It has a very long ribbon-like tongue and enlarged salivary glands.

AARDVARK OR ANTBEAR
(Erdvark)
Orycteropus afer

Plate 37
No. 1

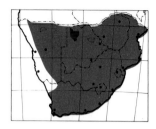

Total length about 1,6 m, mass up to about 65 kg.

Widespread throughout the Subregion except in forest and desert.

The aardvark bears some resemblance to a pig, with its long, tapering muzzle and pale yellowish grey, sparsely haired body. Its shape is, however, unique among African mammals, as it has much bulkier hindquarters than fore-quarters, a thick tapering tail, heavy powerful limbs and long, tubular ears. In outline the body is arched, the highest point above the hind limbs, sloping off gently to the snout and more abruptly to the tail. There are four digits on the front feet and five on the hind. The digits on the front feet are armed with long spatulate claws with sharp edges, those on the hind with shorter, curved, spatulate claws. These claws, backed by pow-erful limbs, give the aardvark its prodigious dig-ging abilities. There is a more profuse covering of hair on the limbs than on the body. The slit-like nostrils are surrounded by a dense mat of hair which, when the nostrils are closed while digging, helps to exclude dust and detritus.

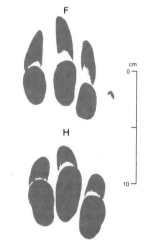

The aardvark is almost exclusively nocturnal, usually occurring singly. It moves up to 15 km in its nocturnal foraging. Its eyesight is poor, but the senses of smell and hearing acute. Apart from exploratory scratchings, it makes three types of excavations: shallow diggings for food, which are not used as refuges; more extensive burrows, which may penetrate several metres into the ground and be used for limited periods, and permanent burrows with extensive tunnels and several entrances, which are used regularly and in which the females give birth to the young. Occupied burrows are character-ised by swarms of small flies inside the entrance. These burrows provide shelter for a wide range of mammals, birds and reptiles. It buries its faeces in shallow scrapes. Ants form a substantial part of the diet, which also includes termites, and, occasionally, other insects. Very little information is available on its reproduction, but it appears to have a single young late in the winter or in early spring, after a gestation period of about seven months. **(S288)**

Order **PROBOSCIDEA**, Family **ELEPHANTIDAE**. The flexible trunk with the nostrils at the end is a characteristic feature of members of this Family, which is represented in Africa by a single species.

AFRICAN ELEPHANT
(Afrikaanse olifant)
Loxodonta africana

Plate 37
No. 2

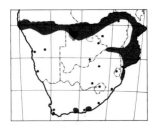

Shoulder height: males up to about 4 m, females about 3 m; mass: males 5 500–6 000 kg, females 3 500–4 000 kg.

Occurs in the northern and northeastern parts of the Subregion, with relict populations in the Addo National Park and in northern Namibia, and about three individuals surviving in the Knysna Forest, Cape Province. Generally associated with savanna woodland, but can adapt to living in arid areas, providing water is available, as it has done in Kaokoland, northern Namibia.

The African elephant hardly requires description, as it is well known even to many people who have never seen it in the wild. It is grey or brownish grey in colour. The trunk, which is a feature, is an extremely versatile organ and can perform most of the operations carried out by the hands in man. With it it plucks its food and conveys it to the mouth, sucks up drinking water, which is pumped into the mouth or over the body as a spray to cool itself, and with the aid of its double-pointed tip it can manipulate even tiny objects. The ears are very large, in an old bull, nearly 2 m in height and 1,2 m broad. They are liberally supplied with blood vessels and when flapped act as convectors, cooling the blood. They express the mood of the individual and when it is enraged they are held outward as it charges. The sides of the face are often marked by dark secretions from the temporal gland. The tusks, which are larger in the bulls than the cows, are ever-growing incisor teeth composed entirely of dentine (ivory). At an early stage they have a cap of enamel which is soon lost. Tuskless elephants of both sexes are known and have a tendency to

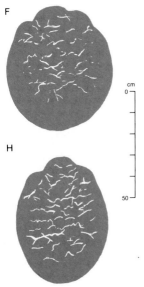

F

H

cm
0

50

Plate 37: **1.** Aardvark (Antbear) (p. 131) **2.** African Elephant (p. 132).

132

37

1

2 ✓

be aggressive. The tusks are used for digging and, in conjunction with the trunk, for breaking down branches for food and in fighting. There are five nails on the front feet and four on the hind. The outer nails are often torn out or worn away. The soles of its feet are cushioned and act as shock absorbers, which allows it to move noiselessly.

Elephants live in family groups consisting of females and their young, these groups often joining up to form large herds. The bulls join these family groups when the females are in oestrus, otherwise living alone or in male herds. The social organisation is matriarchal, based on the lead female in the family group. The bulls fight over females in oestrus and can do each other great damage with their tusks. They both browse and graze, using a very wide range of food plants. They are destructive feeders, pushing over trees to get at the young fresh foliage, and will strip the bark and uproot them to get at the roots. They are second only to man in their capacity to alter their environment. A single young with a mass of about 120 kg may be born at any time of the year. Twins are a rare occurrence. The female leaves the herd to give birth, often accompanied by other females and their offspring to act as guards. The females have a pair of mammae between their front legs and the young suckle with their mouths. The mother is assiduous in her care of her offspring for up to about two years. The young bulls do not compete with older bulls for females until they are about 20 years of age. The females have their first calf at about 11 years of age after a gestation period of 22 months.   **(S289)**

Order HYRACOIDEA, Family PROCAVIIDAE, dassies. This Family is represented in the Subregion by three species: the rock dassie, the yellow-spotted rock dassie and the tree dassie. The first two are associated with rocky terrain, the third is arboreal. They have a pair of enlarged incisor teeth in the upper jaw and two pairs in the lower, which are separated from the cheekteeth by a wide space. The ears are short and barely show above the fur. The limbs are short and sturdy. The soles of the feet are padded with glandular tissue that keeps them moist. The front feet have four digits, the hind three, all armed with a nail, except the inner digit on the hind feet, which is armed with a claw that is used in grooming. They have no external tails. Characteristic features of dassies include the patch of long hair on the middle of the back, overlying a glandular area of the skin. This long hair varies in colour from black to pale yellow, depending on the species involved. Their intestinal tracts are unique among mammals, as they possess a sac attached to the stomach in which bacteria, by fermentation, break down cellulose, and a two-horned caecum whose function is uncertain, but probably acts in absorption. They use latrines, those of the rock dassies often situated below overhanging rocks, those of the tree dassie in the low fork of a tree or on the ground at its base.

ROCK DASSIE　　　　　　　Plate 38
(Klipdas)　　　　　　　　　　No. 2
Procavia capensis

Length of head and body about 54 cm, mean mass: males 3,8 kg, females 3 kg.

Widespread in the Subregion, where there is suitable rocky habitat.

The upper parts of the body vary in colour from greyish brown to yellowish buff, the hair on the glandular patch on the mid-back is black and there is a patch of buffy hair behind the base of the ears. Scattered throughout the coat are long, black tactile hairs.

The rock dassie is diurnal, emerging from its resting places in rocky crevices only after the sun is up and retiring before it sets. Dassies may often be seen sunning themselves on exposed rocks, their compact bodies resembling small rocks. They live in colonies, which vary in size according to the extent of the rocky habitat and the food available. They occasionally share the same rocky habitat with the yellow-spotted dassie, but no interbreeding takes place. In some areas they are predominantly browsers, in other parts grazers and, while they are independent of a water supply, they will drink when it is available. They are fast feeders, the total time expended in feeding being about one hour per day. Litters of up to about three are born in rocky crevices after a gestation period of 230 days. In the Cape Province the young are born in September/October; later in Zimbabwe, about March/April. They are born fully haired with their eyes open and are agile from birth. The sharp bark of the male is the sign for those in his neighbourhood to take cover, but they have a wide repertoire of vocalisations including grunts, growls, wails, twitters and snorts.

(S290)

Plate 38
No. 4

The **Kaokoveld rock dassie** is a subspecies of the rock dassie that is slightly smaller; length of head and body about 46 cm.

Found only in the northwestern parts of Namibia, the coat is brown, yellowish brown or fawn, with white or pale yellow hair on the glandular patch on the mid-back. The hind feet are shorter than those of the rock dassie.

Habitat, food and behaviour are similar to those of the rock dassie. Little is known about its reproduction, but newly born young and pregnant females have been recorded in March. The litters number up to four. **(S291)**

YELLOW-SPOTTED ROCK DASSIE   Plate 38
(Geelkoldas)   No. 3
Heterohyrax brucei

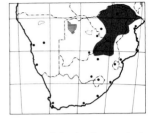

Length of head and body: males about 50 cm, females 52 cm; mean mass 3 kg.

Occurs in the northeastern parts of the Sub-region in rocky habitat similar to that of the rock dassie, in parts sharing this habitat with it.

Colour varies: in the eastern Transvaal the upper parts of the body are dark brown with a reddish tinge, the dorsal spot creamy buff or reddish ochre, the underparts pale yellow. In Zimbabwe it is grey with a brown tinge, the dorsal spot yellowish, the underparts white. Field characters that distinguish it from the rock dassie are the distinct whitish patches above the eyes, the lighter colour of the face and the colour of the dorsal spot, which is never black.

In habitat, food and behaviour it is similar to the rock dassie. In Zimbabwe litters of two are born at any time of the year. The gestation period is not known.   **(S292)**

TREE DASSIE   Plate 38
(Boomdas)   No. 1
Dendrohyrax arboreus

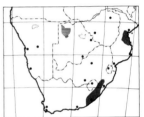

Length of head and body about 50 cm, mass not recorded.

Occurs in three discrete areas of evergreen or riverine forest, one in northern, an other in central Mozambique, and the third in the southeastern parts of the Cape Province, extending into southern Natal.

The coat is greyish with a brown tinge, individuals from the higher rainfall areas tending to be darker than those from the lower. The head is usually darker in colour than the body and the underparts are creamy white to pure white. The fur is much longer than that of the other dassies, giving a woolly appearance. The hair on the dorsal gland is white or off-white and the ears are fringed with whitish hair.

Unlike the other dassies, it is nocturnal, generally solitary and arboreal. It vocalises very loudly in a series of cackling barks and screams and will also

---

Plate 38: 1. Tree dassie (p. 136). **2.** Rock dassie (p. 135). **3.** Yellow-spotted rock dassie (p. 136). **4.** Kaokoveld rock dassie (p. 135).

38

1

2

3

4

growl and grind its teeth. It is more sluggish than the other dassies although agile in the trees, leaping from branch to branch and climbing onto the thinner branches. During the day it rests in hollow trees or among matted creepers or other foliage. Little is known about its diet or reproduction, but it is probably a browser. Litters of up to three are known. **(S293)**

Order PERISSODACTYLA, the odd-toed ungulates. In members of this Order the main mass of the body is borne on the third digit of each foot, either three toes being in contact with the ground, as in the rhinoceroses, or a single toe, as in the zebras. The Order is represented in the Subregion by two Families: the RHINOCEROTIDAE, with two species, the square-lipped (white) and hook-lipped (black) rhinoceros, and the EQUIDAE, the mountain and Burchell's zebras.

HOOK-LIPPED OR BLACK RHINOCEROS

Plate 39
No. 1

(Swartrenoster)
Diceros bicornis

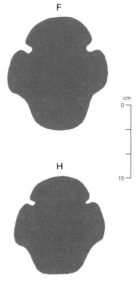

Shoulder height about 1,6 m, mean mass: males about 850 kg, females 880 kg.

At one time occurred on the slopes of Table Mountain and had a wide distribution throughout the Subregion where the only naturally occurring populations today are those in the extreme northwestern parts of Namibia, where very few are left; those in the Hluhluwe-Corridor-Umfolozi game reserve complex in Natal, in the Zambezi Valley in northeastern Zimbabwe and in central Mozambique. Being browsers, their habitat requirements are an adequate food supply in the form of shrubs and trees up to about 4 m high, shade to rest in during the hotter parts of the day, water to drink and to bathe in, and mud in which to wallow.

Characteristic features that distinguish the hook-lipped rhinoceros from its square-lipped relative include the prehensile upper lip, used in grasping food, the shorter head, longer neck and smaller, rounded ears. It lacks the conspicuous hump seen on the shoulders of the square-lipped rhinoceros and is dark grey with lighter underparts. The thick skin has a sparse coat of bristly hairs, there are hairy fringes to the rounded ears and a tuft of black hair on the end of the tail. There are sweat glands scattered over the surface of the skin, which exude droplets of sweat under stress, and it suffers from skin lesions, caused by a filaria parasite. These lesions are blood encrusted and ulcerate and haemorrhage. The horns of the hook-lipped rhinoceros are similar in composition to those of the square-lipped rhinoceros, but the larger front horn is round at the base. The cushioned feet lack the indentation on their rear edge that is manifest in the spoor of the square-lipped rhinoceros.

Through its browsing it prunes bushes so that they become rounded on the sides and top. As it cuts the stems with its premolar teeth, the bushes show no sign of the breaking or tearing that is characteristic of elephant feeding. It is solitary in habits; the only stable bond is between the cow and her calf and this relationship persists into the cow's next pregnancy. Other associations are transitory. The bulls do not defend a territory and generally avoid contact with other adult bulls, but they will fight over an oestrous cow, and there is a high mortality in bulls between eight and ten years of age. Bulls will test the mettle of other bulls by charging at them, screaming, with head lowered, or will buffet them with the horns. Prior to copulation there are complex encounters between the bull and the cow. The latter squirts urine onto the ground which the bull will sniff and then exhibit Flehmen. The bull approaches the cow stiff-legged, his hind legs dragging, and they may spar with their horns, the cow commonly attacking him. A single calf is born at any time throughout the year after a gestation period of about 15 months. The cow suckles her calf for about a year, but it starts to browse on its own at about a few weeks old. She calls it by emitting a high-pitched *mew;* the calf, if it has strayed, calls its mother with a bellowing squeal. Calf mortality is high, caused by predation by lions and hyaenas. **(S296)**

SQUARE-LIPPED OR WHITE RHINOCEROS
(Witrenoster)
Ceratotherium simum

Plate 39
No. 2

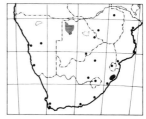

Shoulder height: males about 1,8 m, females about 1,6 m; mass: males 2 000–2 300 kg, females 1 400–1 600 kg.

Today, only occurs naturally in the Hluhluwe-Corridor-Umfolozi game reserve complex in Natal, but has, from surplus populations in this area, been widely translocated to many reserves and to privately owned properties in the Subregion and to zoos overseas. Its habitat requirements include flat terrain, drinking water and mud in which to wallow and areas of palatable short grasses on which to graze.

Grey in colour, the body with a sparse coat of bristly hair, the skin with scattered sweat glands, which exude droplets of sweat when the individual is under stress. The two horns, borne by both sexes, are situated on top of the muzzle and are composed of a mass of tubular hair. They are outgrowths of the skin and are not attached to the skull. The front horn is usually much larger than the hind, its base with a straighter transverse front edge than in the hook-lipped rhinoceros. Characteristic features are the elongated head, pointed ears, wide, squared-off lips, and the distinct hump on top of the shoulders. The feet have three digits, each armed with a stout nail, and are cushioned underneath. The soles have a distinct indentation on the rear edges, which marks in the spoor and distinguishes it from that of hook-lipped rhino, which lacks this feature. The skin is very thick and is folded on the front of the shoulders and at the junctions of the limbs and the body. The senses of smell and hearing are acute but it has poor sight.

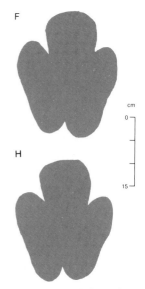

The square-lipped rhinoceros is found in small groups consisting of a territorial bull, subordinate bulls and cows with their offspring. The territorial bulls mark their territories by spray urination and by defecating in latrines along their boundaries. They will charge trespassing bulls or horn clash with them until they move off, but, when a female is in oestrus, fighting may ensue and combatants are sometimes seriously wounded by the horns or by the shoulder battering which takes place. If deposed, the territorial bull may be allowed to remain providing he demonstrates his submissiveness. Square-lipped rhinoceros walk slowly with their heads close to the ground, their nostrils sometimes in contact with it and marking in the spoor, but under stress can gallop at speeds of up to 40 km/h. They mud wallow, especially in hot weather, as a means of thermoregulation and to get rid of ectoparasites. They are grazers and drink water regularly. A single calf is born at any time of the year after a gestation period of 16 months. During the two or three years of association of cow and calf, the calf usually walks in front of its mother and is guided by gentle taps from her horn. **(S295)**

Plate 39: **1.** Hook-lipped (black) rhinoceros (p. 138). **2.** Square-lipped (white) rhinoceros (p. 139).

39

1

2

Family **EQUIDAE**, zebras. In this Family the main mass of the body is carried on the third digit, which is armed with a hoof; only vestiges of the second and fourth digits are present (the splint bones). The males have small canine teeth, which are lacking in the females. The two mountain zebras are dealt with separately, in spite of the fact that they are only subspecies of *Equus zebra*. Both have a distinct dewlap, which is lacking in Burchell's zebra, and narrower body stripes than in that species.

CAPE MOUNTAIN ZEBRA
(Kaapse bergsebra)
Equus zebra zebra

Plate 40
No. 2

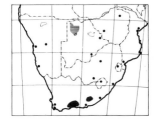

Shoulder height about 1,3 m, mass about 250 kg.

This zebra was saved from extinction only when, in the 1930s, the State proclaimed the farm Babylons Toren, Cradock, a National Park. This area then held five stallions and a mare, but others were introduced from neighbouring farms and today there is a population of over 200. Apart from this there are still small numbers in other mountainous regions in the southwestern Cape Province. They occur in these regions to altitudes of up to 2 000 m where there is grazing, a plentiful water supply and shelter in kloofs and ridges.

The colour of the body is white with transverse black stripes, which are much broader on the rump than on the rest of the body. The legs are striped to a black patch just above the hooves. The black stripes stop at the lower part of the flanks, leaving the underparts of the body white except for the longitudinal black stripe on the middle of the belly and chest. The upper two or three black bands on the rump are exceptionally broad, with no "shadow" stripe between them as in Burchell's zebra. On the top of the rump from the front of the pelvis to the base of the tail the black markings form a characteristic gridiron

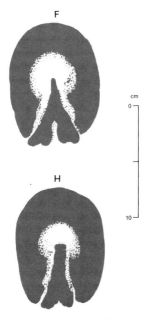

pattern. The tip of the muzzle is black and immediately behind this is suffused with orange on the top and sides. The ears are larger than those of Burchell's zebra.

Social organisation is based on the breeding herd of a stallion, his mares and their foals, which number up to about twelve. This organisation is stable over many years. The stallion may maintain his dominance for up to 15 years. Fights between stallions take the form of rushes towards each other, with head lowered and teeth bared, and kicking. At about two or three years of age the young stallions leave the herds voluntarily and form bachelor herds in which they remain until physiologically mature at about five years of age, when they are ready to become herd stallions.

Cape mountain zebra are diurnal grazers and spend more than half the daylight hours feeding, the remainder of the time resting in the open. During the winter months feeding may continue into the night. The single foal may be born at any time of the year after a gestation period of about 12 months. The foal remains in close association with its mother, who discourages contact between it and other members of the herd. The young females leave the herd at the time of their first oestrus to wander alone until successfully herded by a herd stallion or bachelor. **(S297)**

HARTMANN'S MOUNTAIN ZEBRA
(Hartmann se bergsebra)
Equus zebra hartmannae

Plate 40
No. 1

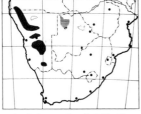

Slightly larger than the Cape mountain zebra; shoulder height 1,5 m; mass: males about 300 kg, females 280 kg.

Occurs in Namibia on the mountainous tran-
sition zone between the Namib Desert and the inland plateau, its distribution today being discontinuous.

Differs from the Cape mountain zebra in having dark and light stripes on the rump about equal in width.

Social organisation and habits are similar to those of the Cape mountain zebra, but Hartmann's tends to be more nomadic, moving from its mountainous habitat to the flats as the food supply diminishes, returning as it improves. The single foal may be born at any time of the year, with a peak in births from November to April. The gestation period is believed to be 362 days.
(S297)

BURCHELL'S ZEBRA ✓
(Bontsebra)
Equus burchelli

Plate 40
No. 3

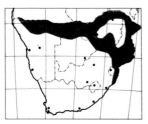

Shoulder height 1,35 m; mass: males about 315 kg, females 300 kg.

Occurs in the northern and northeastern parts of the Subregion in open woodland, open scrub or grassland, seldom more than 10 or 12 km from water.

F

Compared with the mountain zebra, the body stripes are broader and most individuals have yellowish or greyish shadow stripes on the white between the back stripes on the rump. They lack the gridiron pattern on the top of the rump, or it may be confined to the immediate vicinity of the base of the tail, and they have no dewlap. The black body stripes on the flanks continue onto the underparts. There is a well-developed, upstanding black and white mane extending from the head onto the top of the shoulders, and a whisk of long black hair on the end of the tail.

cm

0

H

10

Burchell's zebra live in family groups of a stallion with his mares and their offspring. The size of these groups varies with the density of the population, being larger where the density is greater. When they move the stallion takes up a defensive position at the rear of the group. When attacked by predators the stallion and particularly the mares will vigorously defend the foals by kicking and biting. Under these conditions they vocalise with excited barks.

Family groups often join up to form large herds. In parts of their range they are nomadic, moving from winter to summer grazing areas; in others, however, they are relatively sedentary. They are grazers, though they will browse occasionally, and are partial to areas of short grass, especially where it is fresh and green. The stallions test the reproductive status of their mares by urine smelling and exhibiting Flehmen. Foals may be born at any time of the year, although in the Transvaal there is a peak in births in December/January. The mare remains with the family group to give birth to her single foal, the mother/foal bond being very close-knit. The mares with their foals take the lead when disturbed, protected by those behind and by the stallion at the rear. The foals wean at about 11 months old but may continue to suckle for a time thereafter. The females have one pair of mammae. Burchell's zebra mate freely with donkeys. **(S298)**

Plate 40: **1.** Hartmann's mountain zebra (p. 143). **2.** Cape mountain zebra (p. 142). **3.** Burchell's zebra (p. 143).

40

Order ARTIODACTYLA, the even-toed ungulates. The characteristic feature of members of this Order is that the main mass of their bodies is borne on the third and fourth toes of their feet, these toes equipped with keratinous hooves. In the subregion the Order is represented by four Families: the SUIDAE, pigs; HIPPOPOTAMIDAE, the hippopotamus; GIRAFFIDAE, the giraffe, and the BOVIDAE, the buffalo and 33 species of antelope. The pigs and hippopotamus are non-ruminant members, with simple stomachs. The remainder are ruminants with four-chambered stomachs, rechewing their food or, as it is known, "chewing the cud". The non-ruminant members have at least one pair of upper incisor teeth. In the ruminants the upper incisor teeth are replaced by a tough pad against which the lower incisors occlude.

Family **SUIDAE,** pigs. Members of this Family have stout bodies with thick, tough skin, either sparsely or generously covered with bristly hair. The central pair of digits on the feet are longer than the lateral pair and are armed with well-developed, flattened hooves on which the weight of the individual is borne. The head is elongated and tapers to the snout, which carries an oval, tough, cartilaginous disc, supported internally by the prenasal bone, used in digging. The upper canine teeth protrude from the lips and curve upwards. As the lower canines occlude against the upper canine teeth they are honed so that the tips and edges remain very sharp.

BUSHPIG   Plate 41
(Bosvark)   No. 1
Potamochoerus porcus

Length of head and body about 1,5 m, tail about 40 cm, mass: males up to about 80 kg, females 65 kg.

Occurs in the northern, eastern and southern coastal sectors of the Subregion in forests, thickets, riparian underbrush, reed beds or stands of tall grass where there is water.

Colour varies greatly from reddish to dark brown; some individuals are nearly black. The body is covered with hairy bristles and there is a crest of long, yellowish, erectile hair along the mid-back from the head to the base of the tail, hanging over the sides of the shoulders and body. On the sides of the face, at the level of the angle of the lower jaw, there is a thick patch of long, whitish or yellowish hair, which may extend forwards along the lower edges of the jaw and is very conspicuous in some individuals. The ears are more pointed than in the warthog and have tufts of long hair on the tip and short whitish or yellowish hair along the outer edges. The elongated head is longer than that of the warthog and the face lacks the warts that are such a conspicuous feature of that species.

The bushpig is gregarious, living in sounders of up to about 12, which consist of a dominant boar and sow and other sows, juveniles and piglets. The dominant boar guards and leads the sounder and aggressively drives off other boars from the feeding grounds, with shoulder bristles raised, tail wagging, jaws snapping, often pawing the ground and throwing up dust and clods of earth. When the juveniles in the sounder reach an age of about six months they are driven off by their parents. In areas where they are seldom disturbed they may be seen during the day but where they are subject to control they are largely nocturnal. They can, if wounded or cornered, become dangerous, slashing with their sharp lower canine teeth.

Bushpigs tend to forage in damper places than warthog, rooting up rhizomes of grasses, bulbs and tubers as well as earthworms and the pupae of insects. They eat wild and cultivated fruits, are a pest in agricultural crops, and have been reported to kill and eat chickens, newborn kids and lambs and to take carrion. Litters of three or four, sometimes up to eight, are born during the summer months. The sows construct nests of grass in secluded places, which resemble low hayricks. The young are hardier than those of warthogs. They are rufous brown in colour with conspicuous short yellow or buffy longitudinal elongated blotches. The sows have three pairs of abdominal mammae and apart from suckling the young, leave their care to the dominant boar. **(S299)**

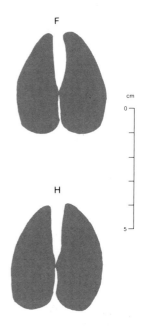

WARTHOG ✓
(Vlakvark)
Phacochoerus aethiopicus

Plate 41
No. 2

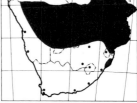

Shoulder height: males about 70 cm, females 60 cm, mass: males up to 104 kg, females 70 kg.

Occurs in the northern, northeastern and eastern parts of the Subregion in open areas of grassland, floodplain, vleis and around waterholes and pans. While it will drink water, it is not dependent on its availability.

The body is grey and is sparsely covered with coarse bristles. The mid-back has a crest of long black, brown or yellowish erectile hair from the ears to the base of the tail, which has a tuft of blackish hair. Characteristic features are the slender legs, the elongated head and in particular the two pairs of conspicuous facial outgrowths of skin, the "warts"; one pair on the sides of the face just below the eyes, the other on the cheeks. These warts are larger in the boars than in the sows. The canine teeth grow out sideways from the jaws; the larger upper pair curling over the upper jaw, the lower occluding against their sides and so remaining honed to sharp points and edges. Their bases are enclosed by thick bony outgrowths of the jaw bones, which cause the snout to broaden out at their level. The ears rise to high, rounded tips.

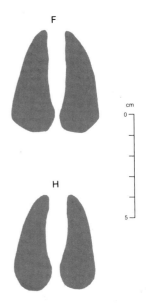

Warthogs are diurnal, resting at night in holes in the ground, usually using deserted antbear holes, which they adjust to their requirements. This type of cover is vital to their survival, affording them protection against adverse climatic conditions, to which they are sensitive, and predators. These holes are used on a "first come first served" basis, although some tenure of holes exists. They are great mud wallowers, the covering affording them protection against biting insects and assisting in thermoregulation. They occur in sounders consisting of a male, a female and her offspring, but the durability of the attachment of the male to his sounder is not known. The sounders are usually larger in the summer, fragmenting at the time of farrowing into smaller sounders. Maternity groups of one or more adult females with their offspring of various age classes are known, as well as bachelor groups of adults and younger males, and solitary males are a common feature. Serious encounters between boars are rare, but a strange boar approaching a male with his sounder may be demonstrated against by the male, who will rush towards him, stiff-legged, without contact, paw the ground or, with the mane erected, will drop on his knees and attempt to push the trespasser away with his head. Group contact is maintained by grunting and they will also snarl and snort under stress.

Warthogs live predominantly on grass but will also root for grass rhizomes and eat bark and wild fruits and occasionally invertebrates and carrion. They prefer to feed in damp areas where the grass grows in lawn-like swards and is fresh and green. They will comb off the flowering and seeding heads of

Plate 41: **1.** Bushpig (p. 146). **2.** Warthog (p. 147).

grasses by pulling the stems through their teeth. They kneel to root for underground food, their knees becoming calloused in the process. Litters of up to about five young are born in holes in early summer after a gestation period of 167 to 175 days. The young huddle on a shelf-like recess in the holes; a precaution against their being drowned if the hole floods. They are very sensitive to low temperatures and require the warm shelter provided by the hole. Mortality is high among the young through climatic factors and predation. The females have two pairs of mammae. **(S300)**

Family **HIPPOPOTAMIDAE**. Two species occur in Africa: the pygmy hippopotamus, in forest in West Africa, and the hippopotamus, widely in aquatic habitat in Sub-Saharan Africa.

HIPPOPOTAMUS Plate 42
(Seekoei) No.2
Hippopotamus amphibius

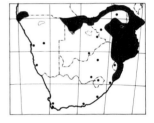

Shoulder height: males about 1,5 m; mean mass: males about 1 500 kg, females 1 300 kg.

At one time, widespread from the Cape Peninsula throughout the Subregion, but is confined today to the northern and eastern sectors in areas where there is adequate open water and adjacent food supplies. It prefers open stretches of permanent water, deep enough to allow it to submerge totally, with gently sloping sandbanks allowing it to rest during the day with its back and top of the head out of the water.

The hippopotamus is characterised by its great size, short, barrel-shaped body, and smooth, naked, greyish black skin, which is pinkish yellow in the skin folds and around the eyes and ears. The head is massive and the eyes, nostrils and relatively small ears are raised above the general level of the upper surface, allowing the hippo to lie in the water with only the top of its head showing and yet retain its senses of sight, smell and hearing. It can remain under water for periods of up to six minutes. It fills its lungs with air and sphincter muscles close the nostrils and ears to prevent the entry of water. The toes are webbed to assist in swimming and it can walk on the bottom under water. The huge permanent incisor and canine teeth are a

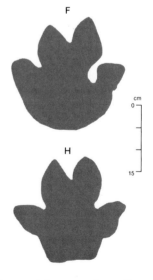

150

feature; the former are round with blunt, rounded tips, the latter triangular in section with very sharp ends which are kept honed by abrasion against the corresponding canine in the other jaw.

The males establish pear-shaped territories, the narrow end where they leave the water, which they will actively defend against trespass from other adult males. The schools, which may number up to about 15 individuals, consist of the territorial male, adult females and juveniles of both sexes. During the day they rest in the water, emerging about sundown to graze on dry land. Their emergence is usually heralded by the characteristic vocalisation of a loud roaring grunt followed by four or five shorter ones, which can be heard over great distances. Young males are evicted from the schools by the territorial male when they reach puberty at about six years old. The territorial male may usually be recognised by his larger size and particularly thick neck. He normally leads the school in their nightly movements to the feeding grounds. Where food is plentiful they tend to remain in the vicinity of the resting pool but they have been known to move up to 30 km nightly where food is not available nearer at hand. In doing so they tend to use established paths which are characteristic, being worn down on either side by the feet, leaving a raised ridge in the middle. Individuals of both sexes are prone to vagrant movements far from their normal haunts.

In territorial encounters the sharp canine teeth inflict serious wounds which can lead to the death of combatants, but cropping of the food is carried out by the hard edges of the lips. They are highly selective grazers, eating about 130 kg of green grass at a feed, and will crop short grass until it assumes a lawn-like appearance. Mating takes place in the water. The single calf is born at any time throughout the year after a gestation period of 225–257 days. The female leaves the school to give birth and hides the calf in the reed beds. At this time she is particularly aggressive and inclined to attack if disturbed. When she rejoins the school after some months, other females will act as "nannies" to her calf when she moves off to feed. The females have a pair of mammae. **(S302)**

Family **GIRAFFIDAE**. Two species occur in Africa: the okapi, in forest in Zaire, and the giraffe, in Sub-Saharan Africa.

GIRAFFE
(Kameelperd)
Giraffa camelopardalis

Plate 42
No. 1

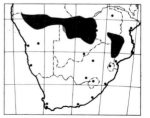

Shoulder height: males about 3 m, females 2,8 m; mass: males about 1 200 kg, females 900 kg.

At one time occurred as far south as the

Orange River, but natural populations are now confined to the northern and northeastern parts of the Subregion. It is associated with various types of woodland that provide the browse plants on which it feeds.

Unmistakable among African mammals, the giraffe is the tallest animal in the world. The body is covered with irregularly shaped patches of chestnut brown, dark brown or nearly black with an off-white or yellowish tinged background. There is a mane of upstanding dark brown hair from the back of the head to the top of the shoulders and a whisk of long black hair on the end of the tail. Adults have a pair of "horns" on the top of the head. Their bony cores are covered with hairy skin except at the calloused blunt tips. The "horns" are not so well developed in the females as in the males, which have in addition a further median "horn" arising on the forehead between the eyes.

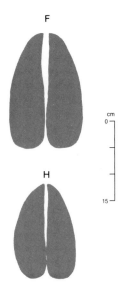

Giraffe are predominantly diurnal, living in small loose herds of males, females and juveniles, which rarely consist of the same individuals for more than a few days at a time. Adult males wander from herd to herd seeking cows in oestrus, which are mated by the highest ranking bulls. Bachelor herds are also found and nursery herds of two or more infants as well as juveniles attended by one or more females are features of the social organisation. The males spar by neck wrestling and fight by swinging blows at each other with the horns. They defend themselves by chop-kicking with the front feet or delivering a swinging kick with the hind feet, actions which have been known to kill attacking lions. Giraffe have a curious gait when walking, the two legs on one side swinging together as they move. They have a lumbering gallop that carries them over the ground very swiftly, the tail swinging in a circular motion. During the heat of the day they rest either in the open or in shade, either standing or lying down. In deep sleep, which lasts only a few minutes at a time, the head is bent back against the body, a posture often seen in the young. Giraffe bellow, grunt or snort when alarmed, *moo* when separated from the herd, and the females whistle to communicate with their young.

They are predominantly browsers, but will occasionally graze on fresh sprouting grasses and, although independent of water, will drink when it is available, straddling the front legs to allow the head to be lowered to the surface of the water. They breed throughout the year. The females produce

Plate 42: **1.** Giraffe (p. 151). **2.** Hippopotamus (p. 150).

42

1

2

their first calf at about five years of age. A single young is produced at a birth, rarely twins. The young is dropped by the female from a standing position, which breaks the umbilical cord. The young lies out, isolated, for up to about three weeks and the female returns regularly to suckle and clean it. The gestation period is 457 days. The young grow fast, females reaching a height of 4,3 m in five years. The females have two pairs of mammae.　　**(S303)**

Family **CERVIDAE**. Members of this Family occur in Europe, Asia and the Americas. It is thought that the fallow deer occurred at one time in North Africa and may have survived in Ethiopia until comparatively recently.

EUROPEAN FALLOW DEER
(Europese takbok)
Cervus dama

There is no record of the original introduction of this species, but it was known as early as 1869 from a herd kept in the grounds of Newlands House, Cape Town. They have adapted well and flourish on privately owned ground in many parts of the Cape Province and Orange Free State, from whence surplus stock continues to be made available for translocation to new areas.　　**(S304)**

Family **BOVIDAE**. Represented in the Subregion by the buffalo and 33 species of antelope. This Family is divided into a series of eight Subfamilies, the members of which have certain attributes in common.

Subfamily **ALCELAPHINAE**. This Subfamily is represented in the subregion by six species: the black and the blue wildebeest, two hartebeests, the tsessebe and the bontebok and blesbok, which are subspecies of *Damaliscus dorcas*. Both sexes have horns, well-developed preorbital glands and pedal glands on the front feet which are rudimentary or absent on the hind feet, and no inguinal glands. The females have a single pair of mammae.

BLACK WILDEBEEST
(Swartwildebees)
Connochaetes gnou

Plate 43
No. 2

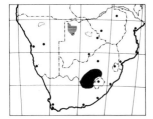

Shoulder height: males about 1,2 m, females about 1,15 m; mass: males about 160 kg, females about 130 kg.
　　A species of open terrain such as the karroid

areas of the Cape Province and the grasslands of the Orange Free State and the Transvaal. In historical times the black wildebeest numbered hundreds of thousands in the central, northern and northeastern parts of the Cape Province, in the Orange Free State and southern Transvaal. By the late 1930s only a few hundred remained, but by judicious conservation their numbers have now increased to the extent that their future is assured and it has been possible to make surplus stock available for translocation widely throughout southern Africa. Only those populations occurring today in the vicinity of the Orange Free State can be considered as arising from naturally occurring populations in the past.

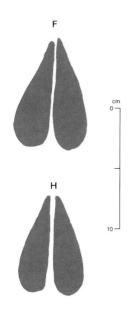

Buffy brown in colour, the old males almost black. The characteristic feature in the field is the long white hair on the tail, which nearly reaches the ground. The head is elongated, with a high, upstanding mane on the neck, a beard of long black hair, long black hair on the chest and a brush of similar coloured hair on top of the muzzle. Both sexes have horns, which arise from expanded bases and sweep downward and forward to curve upward about the end of the muzzle.

The black wildebeest is gregarious, the social organisation involving female and bachelor herds and territorial males, which are closely attached to their territories on a year-round basis. The territorial males mark their territories by spreading secretions of the facial and pedal glands on convenient objects and defend them from trespassers by pawing, kneeling and horning the ground, by vocalising with the characteristic loud *ge-nu* and advertising their ownership by cantering around, stiff-legged. During the rut the female herds are herded within the territory by the territorial male but outside the rut are disregarded. The bachelor herds are loose associations of adult and subadult males and, outside the rut, may be joined by the territorial males who will reoccupy their former territories during it.

The herds are active in the early morning and late afternoon, resting during the day in the open and not seeking shade as do many other bovids. They are predominantly grazers, but will, during the winter months, browse on karroid bushes. They drink water regularly and are dependent on its availability. They are seasonal breeders; the peak of calving takes place during the summer months after a gestation period of 8,5 months. The bond between the female and her single calf is very strong and it remains close to her for the early part of its life, but with the birth of her next calf the female drives it away.   **(S305)**

BLUE WILDEBEEST
(Blouwildebees)
Connochaetes taurinus

Plate 43
No. 1

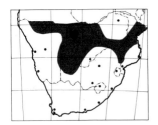

Larger than the black wildebeest; shoulder height: males about 1,5 m, females 1,35 m; mass: males about 250 kg, females 180 kg.

Occurs in the central, northern and north-eastern parts of the Subregion, particularly in open woodland where there is water, on which it is dependent, although in its absence it will eat wild melons.

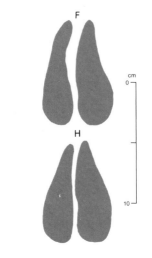

The adult males are dark grey in colour with a silvery sheen, but look black in the distance. On the neck, shoulders and extending back to the mid-body are a series of dark coloured bars, which give a brindled appearance. There is a mane of long dark hair, which droops over the shoulders, a long whisk of black hair on the tail, which nearly touches the ground, and a fringe of long black hair down the middle of the throat. The sides of the face are greyish, sometimes tinged russet, and the adult males have a patch of russet coloured hair on the forehead. The bodies of the females and juveniles are browner than those of the adult males and the russet coloured hair on the forehead is more extensive. Very young individuals are fawn in colour. Both sexes have horns, which are unridged and arise from swollen bosses, sweep outward and slightly downward, then rise upward to inwardly pointed tips, which are often directed slightly backwards. The horns of the females are always lighter in build than those of the males.

The blue wildebeest is gregarious, occurring in herds of up to 30 or in much larger aggregations numbering up to thousands. The social organisation consists of territorial males, female and bachelor herds, but is fluid and only fixed during the rut. At this time the territorial males round up the female herds. Strange adult males are chased off or fighting may ensue, the contestants dropping onto their knees to spar with the horns. The territorial males display to the females by rising on their back legs and holding this stance momentarily before dropping back onto their forefeet. The female herds consist of adult females with their calf of the year. The bachelor herds are loose associations of adult males and juveniles, which live on the least desirable parts of the habitat, separate from that of the female herds.

Plate 43: **1.** Blue wildebeest (p. 156). **2.** Black wildebeest (p. 154).

43

1

2

Whereas in parts of their range blue wildebeest are relatively sedentary, in others they range widely. In Botswana, herds join up to form aggregations of up to tens of thousands, which move widely, perhaps prompted by the occurrence of local rain improving pasture. They may be active throughout the day in cool weather, but usually lie up in shade during the hottest hours of the day and are often active at night. They are grazers with a preference for feeding on short, lawn-like grassland. The main calving season falls between mid-November and February, but may be influenced by prevailing weather conditions. The gestation period is about 250 days. The female may leave the herd to give birth to her single calf. The young females stay with their mothers when they rejoin the female herds, but the young males are evicted from these herds at the age of about two years and join the bachelor herds. **(S306)**

LICHTENSTEIN'S HARTEBEEST Plate 44
(Lichtenstein se hartebees of mofhartebees) No. 2
Sigmoceros lichtensteinii

Shoulder height about 1,25 m; mass: males about 177 kg, females 166 kg.

Represented by a relict population on privately owned land in southeastern Zimbabwe and may still occur in parts of central Mozambique. The National Parks Board has tried to introduce them to the northern parts of the Kruger National Park from Malawi. It is a savanna species particularly associated with the ecotone of open woodland and vleis or grassland where there is surface water, on the availability of which it is dependent.

The upper parts of the body are yellowish tawny in colour, with an indistinct rufous tinged saddle extending from the shoulders to the base of the tail. The chin, the front of the lower parts of the limbs and the tuft of long hair on the end of the tail are black, the base of the tail and the rump white. The face is elongated and there is a distinct hump on the top of the shoulders, which accentuates the slope of the back towards the hindquarters. Both sexes have horns arising

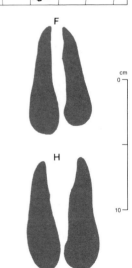

from flange-like bases, bending forward and outwards, then inwards and backwards to diverging tips. Only the immediate vicinity of the flange-like base is ridged.

Occurs in small herds of up to about ten, with seasonal aggregations of much larger numbers. The males are territorial and maintain their territories on a year-round basis. They mark these territories by the creation of latrines and by rubbing their preorbital glands on the ground or on stands of grass that they have vigorously horned and, especially during the rut, will defend them from trespass by other males by viciously attacking them. The horned areas are very conspicuous and may extend over an area of 1,3 square metres, the grass flattened and the soil disturbed. During the rut the males herd females into their territories and endeavour to retain them there, remaining keenly alert to their welfare. They often take up a stance on elevated ground to keep the females and the surrounding terrain in view. The female herds are relatively stable but there is some interchange of adult females with other herds. The bachelor herds live in the less favourable parts of the habitat.

They are almost exclusively grazers and have a preference for areas where the grass is short, especially favouring areas of fresh green sprouting grass after a burn. They have the habit of rubbing their faces on their flanks and after grazing over burnt areas this often leaves a distinct black mark just behind their shoulders which washes away after rain. A single young is born early in summer after a gestation period of 240 days. The territorial male courts his females by approaching them with his nose pointed forward and his tail stiffly horizontal. He may rub his preorbital glands on her rump before mounting. Although the newly born young can follow the mother from birth, she usually beds it down in the open while she grazes with the herd.   **(S307)**

RED HARTEBEEST
(Rooihartebees)
Alcelaphus buselaphus

Plate 44
No. 1

Shoulder height: males about 1,25 m, females about 1,1 m; mass: males about 150 kg, females 120 kg.

Occurs in the central, northern and north-eastern parts of the Subregion and is associated with open grassland and arid scrub, avoiding woodland except in transit.

The colour of the body in adults varies from reddish brown to a yellowish fawn, with a saddle of darker colour from the shoulders broadening towards the base of the tail. This saddle is more distinct in the males than in the females, in which it is sometimes barely perceptible. A characteristic feature of the colour pattern is the well-defined pale yellow or off-white colour of the rump, which looks white in the field. The lower part of the shoulders is

159

suffused with black and this continues down the front of the forelegs either to the knees or, in some cases, to the hooves. The upper parts of the back legs are similarly suffused with black. The forehead is black and there is a patch of reddish brown hair across the face between and in front of the eyes and a black band down the muzzle. These and the other black markings on the body have a plum-coloured iridescence. In some cases, in strong light, the black facial markings shine white, giving the impression of white facial markings. There is a black band on the top of the neck from the top of the head to the shoulders and a whisk of black hair on the end of the tail. The head is elongated and the horns, which are present in both sexes, are mounted on a pedicle on top of the head. Set closely together at the base, the horns rise straight up, curve forward and then backward, almost at right angles. The curved portion is heavily ridged, the ends smooth. The outline of the back is characteristic of members of the genus, the shoulders with a distinct hump, the back sloping towards the tail. The underparts of the body are lighter in colour than the upper.

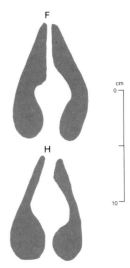

Red hartebeest are gregarious, occurring in herds of up to about 20, which join to form larger aggregations of up to about 300 and at times larger aggregations, which may be due to movements onto preferred feeding grounds. During the rut the males are territorial, herding females into their territories, marking these territories with dung and defending them against male trespassers. The female herds move more widely than the males but may be accompanied by an adult male for an extended period. The bachelor herds consist of males of all ages, and solitary males are not uncommon. Red hartebeest are active in the early morning and late afternoon and they rest during the heat of the day in the open. When disturbed they run off in a bounding gallop and can attain speeds of 60–70 km/h, usually swerving from side to side.

They are predominantly grazers but have been shown to adapt to browsing as well. The territorial males test the reproductive status of females by genital sniffing and court them by advancing towards them with their heads outstretched and ears lowered. They are seasonal breeders; in the Transvaal the

Plate 44: **1.** Red hartebeest (p. 159). **2.** Lichtenstein's hartebeest (p. 158).

44

1

2

main calf crop is born in October/November and in the Kalahari in August, after a gestation period of eight months. The females have their first calf at the age of about three years. After birth the female leaves her calf hidden in tall grass while she rejoins the herd, visiting it to suckle and clean it up. As soon as it is strong enough to follow her, she leads it and rejoins the female herd.

(S308)

BONTEBOK
(Bontebok)
Damaliscus dorcas dorcas

Plate 45
No. 1

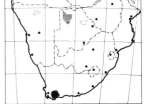

Shoulder height: males about 90 cm; mass: males about 60 kg, the females smaller and lighter in weight.

The bontebok and blesbok are very closely related and are simply subspecies of *D. dorcas,* a species which at one time had a wide distribution in the southern part of Africa, but probably through climatic changes in past geological ages split into two discrete populations. Today bontebok are restricted in their distribution to the southwestern Cape Province, where they occur on a narrow sector of coastal plain within the *fynbos* association, where water and cover are available. Conservation of the small remnant population remaining in the 19th century has led to a great increase in their numbers and allowed a surplus to be made available within recent times to farmers and reserves in this area, their future survival now being assured. They remain, nevertheless, the least common of our southern African antelope.

The colour of the upper parts of the body is rich dark brown, darker on the sides of the head, flanks, top of the rump and upper parts of the limbs, which have a purple sheen. The rump, lower parts of the limbs (except the forelimbs, which have a brown stripe down the front), the base of the tail and the underparts are pure white. The conspicuous white scrotum of the male clearly marks his sex. The terminal part of the tail is brown with long black hair towards the tip. The face, from the forehead to the nostrils, has a white blaze, which is not, in the great majority of individuals, divided between the eyes with a transverse brown band as in the blesbok. Both sexes have ridged horns, those of the females more slender than those of the males. These rise from the head, curve backwards and outwards and then slightly forward to smooth ends.

Bontebok are gregarious animals. The males are territorial, some on a year-round basis, and the territories are defended by ritual displays including head nodding, snorting, bucking and kicking, but rarely by actual encounters. The female herds may wander over the territories of several males but during the

162

rut are herded, tested for their reproductive status by genital sniffing and courted by the approach of the territorial male with muzzle and tail out-stretched. Herds are most active in the early morning and late afternoon, resting during the hottest part of the day clustered together in the shade of thickets. They are almost exclusively grazers, with a preference for feeding on areas of short grass. A single young is born, after a gestation period of between 238 and 254 days, during the months of September to November, with late arrivals up to February. The young females remain with their mother after the new lambs are born, but the males leave them to join the bachelor herds at about a year old. **(S309)**

BLESBOK
(Blesbok)
Damaliscus dorcas phillipsi

Plate 45
No. 2

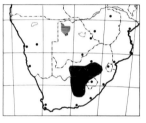

F

Shoulder height: males about 95 cm, mass: males about 70 kg, the females slightly smaller and lighter in weight (about 60 kg).

Occurs in the eastern and northwestern Cape Province, the Orange Free State, the southern Transvaal and marginally in Natal, on grassland where water is available.

The upper parts of the body are reddish brown, lacking the darker areas seen in the bontebok, with an extensive but ill-defined lighter coloured saddle on the back. The white face blaze is, in the majority of individuals, broken between the eyes by a brown transverse band. The patch on the rump is not white, but simply paler than the body colour. The outer surface of the limbs is dark brown. Both sexes have heavily ridged horns, which curve back from the head then swing outwards, the smooth tips curving evenly forward. The upper parts of the ridges are straw coloured, while those of the bontebok are black.

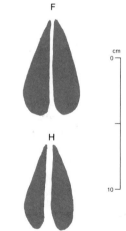

Blesbok are gregarious, occurring in small herds. Their social organisation and habits are similar to those of the bontebok. They are predominantly grazers but will browse and, like the bontebok, have a preference for areas of short grass. A single young is born during the summer, with a peak in births during December, after a gestation period of 240 days. **(S309)**

TSESSEBE
(Tsessebe)
Damaliscus lunatus

Plate 45
No. 3

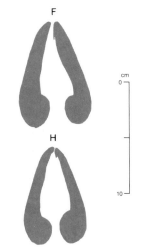

F

H

Shoulder height about 1,3 m; mean mass: males 140 kg, females 126 kg.

The tsessebe has a patchy distribution in the northern and northeastern parts of the Sub-region, and is found on the ecotone of woodland and grassland where water is available.

The body is reddish brown with a distinct purplish sheen. The lower parts of the shoulders, upper parts of the limbs, top of the head and muzzle are suffused with black. The inside of the hind legs and the abdomen are yellowish white, the inside of the front legs above the knees suffused with black, the rump narrowly yellowish white. The lower parts of the limbs below the knees are brownish yellow, the front legs with a narrow band of dark brown down the front. Both sexes have horns, which bend outward in an even curve, then inwards and slightly forwards. They are ridged for nearly their full length, but smooth towards the tips.

Tsessebe occur in small herds, which join up on preferred feeding grounds. The males are territorial and regularly patrol their territories, which they mark by manoeuvring grass stems into their preorbital glands. These stems become covered with a transparent, sticky secretion. They also rub these glands on the ground or on other objects. They defend their territories by advertising their presence on them, by head bobbing or rearing up. Serious fighting is rare, but they will clash horns with trespassers. The female herds remain permanently associated with their territorial male, who will evict young males from them on the approach of the rut. These young males join the bachelor herds that establish themselves on the periphery of the established territories.

They are almost exclusively grazers, showing a preference for tall grasses, but are partial to fresh sprouting grass after a fire. A single calf is born during the early summer months, the bulk of the calf crop appearing in October. The females make no attempt to hide the young, who follow their mothers shortly

---

Plate 45: **1.** Bontebok (p. 162). **2.** Blesbok (p. 163). **3.** Tsessebe (p. 164).

after birth. They often form nursery herds of two to five young when the mothers move off to feed. The yearling males are evicted from the female herds when the new young are about to be born. **(S310)**

Subfamily **CEPHALOPHINAE**. This Subfamily comprises three species: the blue, red and common duiker. They are all small antelope with short straight horns present in both sexes in the blue duiker and in the males of the other two. The females have two pairs of mammae.

BLUE DUIKER
(Blouduiker)
Philantomba monticola

Plate 46
No. 1

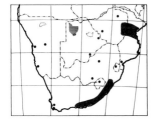

Our smallest antelope; shoulder height: males about 30 cm, females 32 cm; mean mass: males 4 kg, females 4,7 kg.

The blue duiker is specialised in its habitat requirements, being confined to areas of forest, thickets or dense coastal bush, and distribution is therefore governed by the availability of these types of association.

Colour varies with place of origin. Populations in eastern Zimbabwe are dark smoky brown, darker on the head and rump, with a distinct bluish sheen, the underparts white. In the coastal areas of the Cape Province they are dark brown, the limbs rusty reddish brown. Those from coastal Mozambique are much more richly coloured, the upper parts rusty brown, the mid-back dark smoky brown, darkening towards the base of the tail, the limbs light chestnut and the underparts white. Both sexes have short spike-like horns, which lie back from

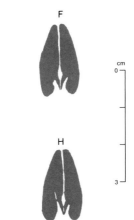

the head in the line of the face and are coarsely ridged basally, with smooth tips. These are usually obscured in the long dark reddish brown hair on top of the head. The preorbital glands are prominent. In the field they give the impression of being higher in the hind-quarters than in the forequarters.

Blue duiker occur singly or in pairs and are difficult to observe as they keep closely to their dense habitat, only approaching open areas with great caution. They feed on fallen leaves and on the fine shoots, leaves and fruits of low-growing underbrush. They are diurnal and territorial. They breed throughout the year with a peak in early summer. A single lamb is born after a gestation of 207 days, and, as a juvenile, has a thick unicolour coat of long, soft hair. **(S311)**

RED DUIKER
(Rooiduiker)
Cephalophus natalensis

Plate 46
No. 2

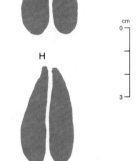

Smaller than the common duiker; shoulder height about 42 cm, mass 10–13 kg.

Occurs only in the eastern and northeastern parts of the Subregion, with an isolated population in the Soutpansberg, northern Transvaal. It is associated with forest, dense thickets, thickly wooded ravines and dense coastal bush where there is surface water.

Deep chestnut red in colour, the flanks and underparts pale chestnut. Mozambique populations are more orange in colour on the upper parts of the body. The sides of the head, the sides of the neck and the inner upper surfaces of the limbs are tawny, the throat white. Both sexes have short, straight horns, which are longitudinally striated basally and smooth towards their tips. They rise from the top of the head, lying back in the line of the face.

The red duiker is a solitary species, pairs associating temporarily, or a female with her young may be seen. It lives in overlapping home ranges. It vocalises with a loud *tchie-tchie* when alarmed and quickly makes for cover if disturbed. The males are thought to be territorial. It eats fallen and growing leaves, wild fruits and seed pods. It breeds throughout the year; gestation is about 210 days. **(S312)**

COMMON DUIKER
(Gewone duiker)
Sylvicapra grimmia

Plate 46
No. 3

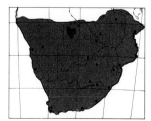

Size varies considerably; shoulder height: males about 50 cm, females 52 cm; mass: males 15–18 kg, females 16–21 kg. Females from Botswana attain masses of up to 25 kg.

167

Widespread throughout the whole of the Subregion and catholic in its habitat requirements, being found practically anywhere there is some cover in which to rest and where the vegetation provides browse. It is independent of water. Colour varies considerably. The upper parts of the body in some areas are greyish, in others reddish yellow. The underparts are usually white but may be grey or tinged reddish. The forehead is usually darker and redder than the upper parts of the body. A distinct black band on top of the muzzle may be restricted to the immediate vicinity of the nostrils or run from them to the forehead. The males have a tuft of long black or dark brown hair between the horns. Only the males have the short, straight horns, which are heavily ridged towards their bases, arising close together on the head and diverging outwards with a slight backward slope. The preorbital glands are conspicuous.

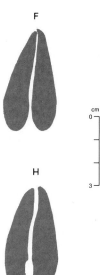

Although generally solitary, pairs associate at the time of mating and females move with their offspring. The main periods of activity are the early morning and late afternoon, extending well into the hours of darkness. They rest in the shelter of bushes or in tall grass. When disturbed they plunge off to safety, usually pausing momentarily to look back for the cause of the disturbance. They are almost exclusively browsers, rarely eating grass, and will feed on the leaves, twigs, flowers, fruits and seeds of a wide variety of plants. They will also dig for roots and nibble on the bark of trees, and have been known to eat mushrooms, young birds, lizards and caterpillars. The young are born at any time of the year, usually a single young at a birth, rarely twins. The gestation period is 190 days and females can conceive at the early age of eight to nine months. The female hides the newly born young in cover and the young can run actively within 24 hours of birth, maturing rapidly to approximately adult size at six to seven months of age. **(S313)**

Subfamily **ANTELOPINAE**. This Subfamily is divided into two Tribes: the ANTELOPINI with one species, the springbok, and the NEOTRAGINI with seven species, the klipspringer, Damara dik-dik, oribi, steenbok, grysbok, Sharpe's grysbok

---

Plate 46: **1.** Blue duiker (p. 166). **2.** Red duiker (p. 167). **3.** Common duiker (p. 167).

and suni. In the Antelopini both sexes have horns and the females one or two pairs of mammae; in the Neotragini the females are hornless and have a single pair of mammae.

SPRINGBOK

(Springbok)
Antidorcas marsupialis

Plate 47
No. 2

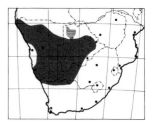

F

Shoulder height about 75 cm; mean mass: males 41 kg, females 37 kg.

Occurs in the northwestern parts of the Sub-region on arid open grassland and semi-desert scrub, avoiding thick woodland, extensive areas of tall grass and rocky hills.

The upper parts of the body are a bright cinnamon brown colour with a characteristic dark reddish brown horizontal band along the flanks, separating the reddish brown colour of the upper parts from the pure white underparts. The centre of the rump is white and this colour continues forward on the lower back to tail out into a dorsal crest of long erectile white hair on the back, which covers a glandular area of skin. The face is white with a reddish brown line running from the eyes to the corner of the mouth and a similarly coloured patch on the forehead. The ears are outstandingly long, narrow and pointed, the neck long for the size of the body, the legs long and slender. Both sexes have lyrate horns, those of the males heavier than those of the

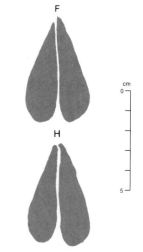

H

females. Rising from above the eyes, they slope backwards, diverging outwards and curving sharply inwards to hooked tips. They are heavily ridged for over half their length and are smooth towards the tips.

Springbok both browse and graze and will drink where water is available but can subsist without it by obtaining their moisture from their food. They are most active in the early morning and late afternoon, and some part of the herds are active throughout the day, but they usually rest in the open during the hottest hours. They will dig for succulent roots in arid areas. When suddenly alarmed they may leap into the air, up to 2 m off the ground, which takes them forward over considerable distances. Stotting is a spectacular action that takes place when they are being chased or are under stress. With

---

Plate 47: **1.** Klipspringer (p. 172). **2.** Springbok (p. 170).

170

the back arched, the dorsal crest of white hair erected and the head held stiffly downward, the individual leaps off the ground, landing on all four feet simultaneously and progressing in a series of these bounds. The males are territorial, but not permanently throughout the year. The social organisation consists of mixed herds numbering into the hundreds and consisting of adults and juveniles of both sexes, and bachelor herds of adult males, sometimes accompanied by a few adult and juvenile females. During the summer, numbers of mixed herds may join up to form much larger herds and at times ever larger aggregations, which have nomadic tendencies. These "treks", as they are called, in historical times involved such large numbers that they covered square kilometres of country, the mass moving in a set direction.

The territorial males herd females and endeavour to hold them within their territories. They test them for signs of oestrus by urine sniffing and Flehmen and court them by approaching at a bouncy trot, tossing their heads. At close quarters the male swings his front leg from side to side as if to tap the female's back leg. Mating may take place at any time throughout the year. The main lamb crop is born during the summer in summer rainfall areas and in winter in winter rainfall areas. The gestation period is 24 weeks. The female hides her single newly born lamb in tall grass, where it remains for a day or two. **(S314)**

KLIPSPRINGER

(Klipspringer)

Oreotragus oreotragus

Plate 47
No. 1

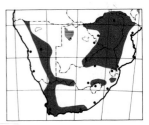

Shoulder height about 60 cm; mean mass: males 10,6 kg, females 13,2 kg.

The klipspringer is restricted by its habitat requirements and its distribution is scattered and discontinuous, in rocky areas.

Unique among African antelopes in having a coat of spiny bristles that are hollow, flattened and springy in texture, acting as an insulator to extremes of heat and cold and as a means of conserving body moisture. Because of these properties, the hair was at one time greatly in demand as a stuffing for saddles. Colour varies depending on place of origin: individuals from the southwestern Cape Province are yellow, speckled with brown; in the Transvaal they are bright golden yellow, speckled with black, and

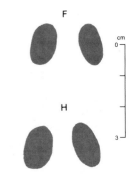

172

in western Zimbabwe they are greyer and duller, the underparts white. In southern Africa only the males have the spike-like horns, which rise parallel to each other with a slight forward curve towards the tips. In Tanzania both sexes have horns. The horns are ridged for about a third of their basal length and are smooth towards the tips.

Klipspringer commonly occur in pairs, or a pair and a juvenile, which sometimes join others to form temporary groups of up to about six, usually on feeding grounds. They are adept at moving in their rocky habitat, their peg-like hooves have resilient centres and hard rims to provide grip in leaping from rock to rock. The pairs are territorial and their territories are marked by glandular secretions from the preorbital gland, into which they will manoeuvre a twig to cover it with a black tarry substance, and by the creation of scattered latrines. They defend these territories mainly by displaying themselves, often standing on a pinnacle of rock with their four feet together, but they will also attack trespassers, combatants often being severely wounded. Klipspringer have a loud, high-pitched alarm call and pairs often call in a duet when predators are in the vicinity. It is a repetitive and highly directional sound and has the function of communicating their alertness to the predator more than warning other klipspringers. They are predominantly browsers and will often stand on their hind legs to reach wild fruits or other food. They will drink when water is available but are generally independent of it, getting the moisture they require from their food. They breed throughout the year. A single young is born in rocky shelter and remains there until it is able to move with its mother. The gestation period is about six months. **(S315)**

DAMARA DIK-DIK
(Damara dik-dik)
Madoqua kirkii

Plate 48
No. 1

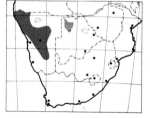

Shoulder height about 40 cm, mass 5 kg.

Restricted to the northern and central parts of Namibia in dense woodland with a well-developed scrub undercover and in thickets on hard, stony ground.

The upper parts of the body are yellowish grey in colour, the hair with a subterminal pale yellow ring and dark tip, which gives the coat a grizzled appearance. The face and crown of the head are a pale rusty colour, paler on the sides of the neck, but richer on the shoulders and flanks. The underparts are pure white. There is a tuft of long orange-brown hair on the forehead, which is erected under stress or during courtship. The eyes are ringed with white hair. A characteristic feature is the elongated, mobile proboscis-like snout, which lacks a rhinarium, the nostrils being plain openings, and there are large, conspicuous preorbital glands on the sides of the muzzle. The hooves have rubbery pads at the back, which lie in contact with the ground and act as shock absorbers. Only the males have the short, spike-like horns, which are ridged and longitudinally grooved and lie in the line of the face.

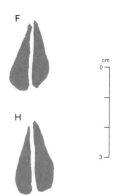

The Damara dik-dik occurs either singly, in pairs or in family parties of a male, a female and her offspring in small territories. Family parties sometimes temporarily join others to form groups of up to six. They are shy and, when alarmed, vocalise with an explosive whistle and run for cover, disappearing in the densest part of the undergrowth. They are active around sunrise and sunset, with some nocturnal activity, and rest during the day, standing or lying down in shady cover. They defecate in communal dung heaps and, after using these, they move to the nearest clump of grass on which they wipe their preorbital glands, leaving a black, tarry secretion that builds up into blobs by constant marking. They are predominantly browsers although, during the summer, they graze on the leaf tips of grasses. They are independent of water but will drink if it is available. A single young is born during the summer. The males court the females by approaching them with the head held low, the nose forward and the crest of long hair on the forehead fully erected. The gestation period is about six months, and the young stay with their mothers until the next offspring is born.   **(S316)**

ORIBI
(Oorbietjie)
Ourebia ourebi

Plate 48
No. 3

Shoulder height about 60 cm, mass about 14 kg.

Occurs in isolated areas in the northern, eastern and southeastern parts of the Subregion. It inhabits open grassland, where the grass is up to about 40 cm high, avoiding areas of tall grass and woodland (which, however, it will use marginally for the cover it provides).

The colour of the upper parts of the body is yellowish rufous, contrasting with the pure white of the underparts, which extends over the rump to the

---

Plate 48:   1. Damara dik-dik (p. 173).   **2.** Steenbok (p. 176).   **3.** Oribi (p. 174).

base of the tail and high onto the front of the chest. The coat is fine and silky and inclines to curliness on the back. There is a marked difference between the shorter summer coat and the longer and more shaggy winter coat. The face is characteristically marked with two white blazes, one on either side of the snout, and there are distinct white crescent marks above the eyes, extending slightly forward onto the face. Oribi have longer, thinner necks than steenbok and can immediately be distinguished from them as the top of their tails are black whereas in steenbok they are the same reddish colour as the body. Only the males have horns, which rise straight up from the head with a slight forward curve towards the tips. Set widely spaced at the base like those of the steenbok, they differ in being strongly ridged towards the base.

F

H

cm
0

3

Oribi occur solitarily, in pairs or family parties of a male and up to two females and their offspring. The family parties sometimes join up temporarily to form small herds of up to about 12. The males are territorial, at least during the rut, and defend their territories by advertising their presence and by marking with glandular secretions. They mark on grass stems by nipping off the top and rubbing the cut stem with the preorbital glands, which leaves a small amount of black secretion on it. When alarmed they vocalise with a snorting whistle and bound off stotting with a "rocking-horse" action, holding their heads erect, then usually pausing in flight to seek the source of the disturbance. Oribi are very selective feeders and have a preference for fresh sprouting grass after a burn. The main lambing season is in the summer, while odd births are recorded at other times of the year. The mother hides the single young in the grass for 3 to 4 months and returns to suckle it after feeding. The gestation period is 210 days. **(S317)**

STEENBOK

Plate 48
No. 2

(Steenbok)
Raphicerus campestris

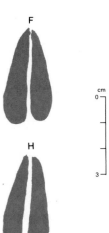

A small, graceful antelope; shoulder height about 52 cm, mass 11 kg.

Widespread throughout the Subregion except in parts of the extreme northeast. It inhabits open grassland where there is some cover in the form of stands of tall grass, bushes or scrub, and avoids densely wooded areas, forests and desert or rocky hills and mountain slopes.

The upper parts of the body vary in colour from rufous brown to reddish, the underparts pure white. The pointed muzzle is dark on top and more richly rufous in colour than the body. Some individuals have a distinct black Y-shaped marking on the forehead, the long axis lying on top of the muzzle. Only the males have horns, which rise vertically from the head and are ridged towards their bases, but are otherwise smooth, with a tendency to curve forward towards the tips. The hooves are narrow and sharp pointed, a feature that marks in the spoor.

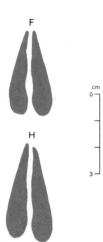

Steenbok lead solitary lives except at the time of mating or when a female has a lamb. They are active around sunrise and sunset and, during cool, overcast weather, throughout the day, and will move and feed after dark. They have well-defined territories, which they mark by establishing latrines near the perimeters and by marking with the secretions of the preorbital, throat and pedal glands. Both sexes defend their territories against trespassers, mainly by advertising their presence within them. When defecating or urinating they clear a spot with their front hooves and carefully cover it up by scraping soil over it, again with the front hooves. During the heat of the day, they lie up well hidden and when flushed run off with their heads thrust forward, often pausing in flight to look back for the cause of the disturbance. Under severe stress they will hide in holes in the ground. They browse and graze, and are selective feeders. The single lamb may be born at any time of the year. The gestation period varies from 168 to 173 days. **(S318)**

GRYSBOK
(Grysbok)
Raphicerus melanotis

Plate 49
No. 3

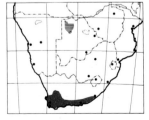

Shoulder height about 54 cm, mass about 10 kg.

Occurs only in the southwestern and southern parts of the Cape Province in thick scrub bush, particularly along the lower levels of hills or mountain slopes, in kloofs and in coastal bush.

Reddish brown in colour, the coat sprinkled with white hairs, giving it a grizzled appearance; the face, neck, legs and flanks are yellowish brown, the underparts buffy. The ears are large, greyish on the back and buffy white inside, and the short tail is the same colour as the body. Only the males have horns, which rise vertically from the head with a slight forward slant and are inconspicuously ridged towards the base.

Grysbok occur solitarily, in pairs or a female with her offspring. They are territorial. They are browsers, taking leaves and wild fruits and can be a problem species in vineyards, as they nibble off the young shoots. Predominantly nocturnal, they are active around sunrise and sunset, and lie up during the day in thick cover. Young are born throughout the year with a peak from September to December. **(S319)**

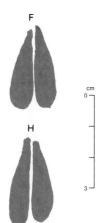

SHARPE'S GRYSBOK

Plate 49
No. 2

(Sharpe se grysbok)
Raphicerus sharpei

Shoulder height: males about 45 cm, females 50 cm; mean mass: males 7,3 kg, females 7,7 kg.

Occurs in the eastern and northeastern parts of the Subregion in areas of low-growing scrub and grass, often around the base of koppies and stony ridges.

Rich reddish brown in colour, the coat liberally sprinkled with white hairs, giving it a grizzled appearance. The sides of the face, outer parts of the limbs, the forehead and upper parts of the muzzle are yellowish brown, the top of the muzzle with a dark band from the rhinarium to just in front of the eyes, which have a white ring encircling them. The underparts of the body are buffy white. Only the males have the short straight horns, which slope back from the head, tapering abruptly to sharp points. The hair on

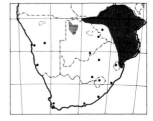

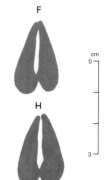

Plate 49: **1.** Suni (p. 180).   **2.** Sharpe's grysbok (p. 178).   **3.** Grysbok (p. 177).

the upper parts of the body is longer than in the steenbok, and the false hooves present on the hind legs of its near relative, the grysbok, are absent. Preorbital, preputial and pedal glands are present.

Sharpe's grysbok occur solitarily, in pairs or a female with her offspring and are active around sunrise and sunset and at night, lying up during the heat of the day in thick cover. They are difficult to observe as they live in a concealing habitat and are inclined to lie up tightly, but when a clear view is possible they are seen to hold their heads low, the outline of the back giving the impression that the hindquarters are higher than the shoulders and are drawn in to the body. When disturbed they run off, crouching low, and are usually obscured by the low scrub and grass, which distinguishes them from the duiker or steenbok, as neither of these crouches in similar circumstances. They are predominantly browsers, but will also eat grass. The single young may be born at any time throughout the year. The gestation period is 7 months. **(S320)**

SUNI
Plate 49
(Soenie)
No. 1
Neotragus moschatus

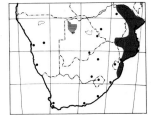

A tiny antelope; shoulder height about 35 cm, mean mass: males 5,1 kg, females 5,5 kg.

Occurs only in the extreme eastern and north-eastern parts of the Subregion. It is associated with dry woodland with thickets and under-brush, riparian scrub or dry scrub along drainage lines, and is independent of surface water.

Colour is a rich reddish brown, slightly speckled with buff; the mid-back from the neck to the base of the tail is darker than the flanks and limbs, the underparts are white. The hair on the forehead and top of the head is dark reddish brown, the sides of the face lighter in colour than the body; there is a whitish patch above the eyes, and broad, rounded ears. Only the males have horns, which are flattened in section and heavily ridged for most of their length.

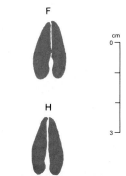

Suni occur solitarily, in pairs or in family groups consisting of a male or female and her offspring. They are shy and wary and if disturbed will freeze before bounding away, vocalising with a high-pitched *chee-chee,* to disappear in the nearest thick cover. They use communal latrines and rest during the heat of the day in the same place, which they use over long periods. The males are territorial, marking their feeding areas with secretions from preorbital glands. They eat mainly fallen leaves but will browse and eat wild fruits and mushrooms. A single young is born at any time of the year after a gestation of about 7 months. **(S321)**

Subfamily **AEPYCEROTINAE**. This Subfamily is represented in the Subregion by a single slenderly built, gazelle-like species, the impala, which is a medium-sized antelope, the males with lyrate horns, the females hornless. They have no facial, pedal or inguinal glands but have conspicuous black tufts of hair on the hind legs arising from metatarsal glands. The females have two pairs of mammae.

IMPALA
(Rooibok)
Aepyceros melampus

Plate 50
No. 1

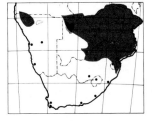

Shoulder height: males about 90 cm, females 85 cm, mean mass: males 55 kg, females 40 kg.

Widespread throughout the northeastern parts of the Subregion, with an isolated population in the northwestern parts of Namibia (the black-faced impala). Impala are associated with light open woodland where there is surface water; the black-faced impala prefers dense riverine associations and is similarly dependent on the availability of water.

Impala are graceful antelopes, with shiny reddish coats and long slender legs, the flanks pale fawn tinged reddish, the underparts pure white. They have white patches above the eyes, white throats, a dark brown or nearly black patch high up on the forehead, and conspicuous patches of black hair just above the ankles on the hind legs, overlying glandular areas in the skin. A characteristic feature is the distinct black bands on either side of the rump, running from near the base of the tail down the back of the thighs, which are flanked with pale fawn areas against which these black bands stand out con-

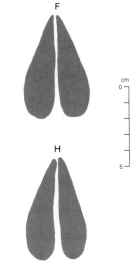

spicuously. The top of the tail is broadly black, and a fine line of this colour continues forward onto the top of the hindquarters; the underparts of the tail are white. The ears are white inside, with contrasting black tips. Only the males have the lyrate shaped horns, which are strongly ridged for about two-thirds of their length and are smooth towards the tips.

Impala occur in herds of up to about 20 and larger aggregations of up to about 100 during the cold, dry months. The males are territorial only during the rut in autumn, when they establish territories that they mark by forehead and facial rubbing on grasses and twigs. They vigorously defend their territories against trespassing males by vocalising, chasing and other displays, including snorting, strutting, head bobbing, horn clashing and head pushing, which may lead to short bouts of serious fighting, followed by roaring. The nursery herds of adult females and juveniles of both sexes are herded by the territorial male, who tests the reproductive status of the females by genital smelling and licking. The males court the females by approaching them with lowered head, the nose pointed towards them. Bachelor herds of adult and juvenile males are a common feature of the social organisation of the species. At the time of the rut the territorial males evict other males from their territories and these join the bachelor herds. If suddenly disturbed, the herds break up wildly in all directions, leaping over bushes and imaginary objects, until they rejoin and stream off to safety. In leaping they appear to float through the air, their bodies in a graceful arc which may carry them over distances of up to 10 or 12 m.

Impala both browse and graze, this varying with the locality and season of the year. The whole of the lamb crop is born within a narrow period of a few weeks, usually early in the summer, but varying with the locality. The single newly born young remains hidden in cover for a few days, but is capable of following its mother shortly after birth. Gestation is 194 to 200 days.

The black-faced impala of northwestern Namibia differs from the impala in that it is heavier and darker in colour, the upper parts of the body are duller brown with a distinct purplish black sheen, there is a distinct purplish black band on top of the muzzle from near the nostrils to the top of the head and dark bands from the base of the ears to the eyes, tapering out on the cheeks. The tips of the ears are more extensively black, the tail longer than in the impala and much bushier.   **(S322)**

Subfamily **PELEINAE**. This Subfamily is represented in the Subregion by a single species, the grey rhebok, a medium-sized antelope, the males with short, straight horns. They have no facial or inguinal glands, but pedal glands are present and the males have preputial glands. The females have two pairs of mammae.

Plate 50: **1.** Impala, male and female (p. 181). **2.** Grey rhebok (p. 184).

50

1

2

GREY RHEBOK
(Vaalribbok)
Palea capreolus

Plate 50
No. 2

Shoulder height about 75 cm, mass about 20 kg.

Found only within the limits of the Subregion, from the southwestern Cape Province to the central Transvaal. It is associated with rocky hills and mountain slopes with a good grass cover and is independent of a water supply.

Greyish brown in colour with white underparts, the front of the legs darker in colour than the body. The eyes have a conspicuous white ring around them and there is some white on the sides of the muzzle and chin. It has a long, slender neck and long, narrow, pointed ears. Only the males have the short, upstanding horns, which have a slight forward curve and are ringed for about half their length.

Grey rhebok live in small family herds of up to about 12, which sometimes join up to form larger temporary aggregations. The males are territorial and defend at least part of the home range, the young males leaving the family herd at the lambing time, but not joining up to form bachelor herds as do other species. Defence of the territory takes the form of displays involving exaggeratedly slow movements towards the trespasser, displaying laterally and frontally towards him, accompanied by snorting and foot stamping. They are active throughout the day, resting in shade during the hottest hours.

They are accomplished active leapers, jumping over barriers with ease, and when disturbed move off with characteristic "rocking-horse" movements, displaying the white underside of the tail. Grey rhebok are browsers. The territorial males tests the reproductive status of the females by genital sniffing, courting them by tapping the insides of their back legs with his foreleg. The gestation period is 261 days. A single lamb is born during the summer. **(S324)**

Subfamily **CAPRINAE**. Members of this Subfamily resemble goats but have anatomical characters of both antelopes and goats.

HIMALAYAN TAHR
(Himalaya tahr)
Hemitragus jemlahicus

The Himalayan tahr was accidentally introduced to Table Mountain by the escape of a pair from the Groote Schuur Zoo in the 1930s. By 1972 the population was estimated to number over 300, and as they are destructive of the habitat, the herds tending to remain for long periods in restricted areas, they posed a threat to the unique flora and conservation status of the mountain. A control programme was initiated by the Cape Department of Nature

Conservation, which reduced the population to under 100 by 1981. Control continues and the situation is being carefully monitored by this Department.

(S323)

Subfamily **HIPPOTRAGINAE**. This Subfamily is represented in the Subregion by three species: the roan, sable and gemsbok. They are large antelope with pedal glands on all four feet, no inguinal glands, with the facial glands absent or at most slightly developed. The females have two pairs of mammae.

ROAN
(Bastergemsbok)
Hippotragus equinus

Plate 51
No. 1

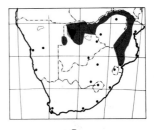

A large antelope, surpassed in size only by the eland; shoulder height: males 1,4 m; mass: males about 270 kg, females 230 kg.

Occurs in parts of the northern and north-eastern sectors of the Subregion in open woodland where there are extensive areas of medium to tall stands of grass and where open water is available. It is sensitive to changes in the habitat, and bush encroachment or over-utilisation by other species can render grassland unsuitable for it.

The body is greyish brown, tinged with strawberry, the face black or dark brown with strongly contrasting white facial markings. The limbs are darker in colour than the body, the upstanding hair of the mane brown at the base and black tipped, the forehead reddish. The ears are very long and have dark brown tassels of hair at their tips. The tail has long black hair at the tip. Both sexes have horns, those of the females more lightly built than those of the males. Round in section, they curve evenly backwards from the top of the head and are heavily ridged except towards the tips.

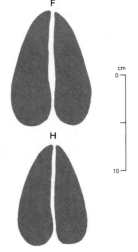

Roan live in herds of up to about 12, which may aggregate to form larger herds of up to 80. The social organisation consists of lone bulls, nursery herds of females and juveniles accompanied by a dominant bull, and bachelor herds of adult and juvenile males. The adult males with the nursery herds are not considered to be territorial but they do defend their females from the attentions of other adult males. Should a strange male attempt to oust the dominant male from a herd he will vigorously defend himself and his females and high intensity fighting ensues, with horn clashes and head pushing, which may continue for long periods. Submission of a contestant is demonstrated by lowering the head.

The herds have activity zones which they may occupy for a number of years. They are predominantly grazers, but will browse. Active around sunrise and sunset, they rest during the heat of the day in shade. The dominant male tests the female's urine for signs of her being in oestrus and exhibits Flehmen. He courts her by gently tapping her abdomen with his foreleg inserted between her hind legs. The calves may be born at any time of the year after a gestation period of 276-287 days. The female leaves the herd to give birth. The calves are rich rufous in colour, with facial markings like the adults. **(S325)**

GEMSBOK

(Gemsbok)

Oryx gazella

Plate 51

No. 2

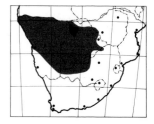

Shoulder height: males 1,2 m, females 1,1 m; mass: males about 240 kg, females 210 kg.

Occurs in the arid central and northeastern parts of the Subregion in open country.

The upper parts of the body are pale fawn grey in colour, with characteristic black bands down the mid-back, the throat, along the lower flanks and on the upper parts and front of the lower parts of the limbs. There is a black patch on top of the hindquarters and the tail is black, with a tuft of long black hair on the tip. The face is marked with black and white, the underparts are white and there is a pale off-white patch on the rump. Both sexes have rounded horns, which rise straight upwards from the head, or with a slight backward curve, ridged for two-thirds of their length and smooth towards the tips. The horns of males are usually slightly heavier and shorter than those of females.

Gemsbok live in herds of about eight which tend to split in the dry season into twos and threes, dispersing to find food. The males are

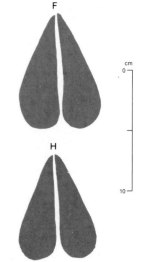

F

H

cm
0 —

10 —

Plate 51: 1. Roan (p. 185). **2.** Gemsbok (p. 186). **3.** Sable (p. 188).

51

1

2

3

males are territorial but more tolerant of other adult males than most territorial species. Their territories are very large, their boundaries marked with piles of dung, and are defended mainly by demonstrative threats, including pawing and horning of shrubbery, and violent clashes. The nursery herds of females and juveniles are herded into his territory by the territorial male, who courts the females in oestrus by tapping them between and on the sides of their hind legs with his foreleg, after he has tested their urine by inserting his nose in the female's urine stream and then exhibited Flehmen. Solitary non-territorial males occur commonly, bachelor herds of two or three adult and juvenile males more rarely.

Gemsbok possess adaptations to allow them to withstand high ambient temperatures. The carotid artery, for example, is broken up into smaller vessels where blood to the brain is cooled by venous blood from the nasal passages and by air circulating over the vessels in panting. Gemsbok are predominantly grazers, but will browse when grass is scarce, and obtain moisture by digging up succulent roots and rhizomes. A single young is born at any time of the year, with a peak in early summer in the Transvaal and later, about December to March, in Botswana, after a gestation period of about 264 days. The newly born young conceal themselves in tall grass or undergrowth and the female joins its young only to suckle and clean it. **(S327)**

SABLE
(Swartwitpens)
Hippotragus niger

Plate 51
No. 3

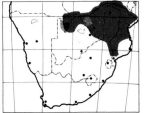

Shoulder height: males 1,35 m; mass: males about 230 kg, females 220 kg.

Occurs in the northern and northeastern parts of the Subregion in open woodland, and is dependent on the availability of water.

The old adult males are black on the upper parts of the body, the females dark brown, nearly black, both with white underparts, distinctive white facial markings, long russet-backed ears and upstanding manes extending from the back of the head to the shoulders. Both sexes have horns, which sweep back in an even curve from the head and are laterally compressed and heavily ridged. The horns of the females are more slender and less sweepingly curved than those of the males.

Sable live in herds of up to 30 and aggregations of up to 200 have been recorded. Their social organisation consists of territorial males, nursery herds of adult and juvenile females and juvenile males, and bachelor herds of non-territorial males and juvenile males. Breeding males establish small terri-

188

tories of 30 to 40 ha during the rut which they defend vigorously by intimidatory displays or fighting, involving bellowing, horn clashing and slashing which can lead to the death of combatants. Outside the rut they move with the herds. Juvenile males in the nursery herds are evicted by the territorial bulls at about three years of age and then join bachelor herds. One or more females may become dominant in the nursery herd and take the lead in its organisation.

Sable are grazers but browse to a greater extent when the nutritional value of the grass drops off at the end of the dry season. They are seasonal breeders, the young being born late in the summer season. A single calf is born, which conceals itself in thick underbrush. The juveniles are reddish brown in colour, the facial markings indistinct. **(S326)**

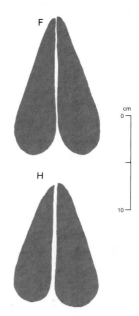

Subfamily **BOVINAE**. This Subfamily is represented in the subregion by six species: the buffalo, kudu, sitatunga, nyala, eland and bushbuck. The famales all have two pairs of mammae.

✓BUFFALO
(Buffel)
Syncerus caffer

Plate 52
No. 2

Very large; shoulder height 1,4 m; mass: males average about 800 kg, females 750 kg.

In historical times the buffalo had a wide distribution in southern Africa, but today it is found only in the northern and eastern parts of the Subregion, with a relict population in the Addo National Park in the eastern Cape Province. Habitat requirements include a plentiful supply of grass, shade and water.

Buffalo are heavily built animals, ox-like in general appearance. The old males are black, the females tinged reddish brown, the body with a sparse covering of hair. Both sexes have horns, those of the males more massive than those of the females. From massive rugose bosses on the front of the head they swing outwards and downwards, then curve upwards and inwards, and usually slightly backwards towards the tips. The limbs are heavily built, the ears large and tipped and fringed with hair.

Buffalo occur in huge herds numbering up to thousands, which are subject to seasonal movements from which smaller herds temporarily split off. Old and juvenile bulls may leave the herds and form bachelor groups and solitary old bulls are frequently seen. Adult bulls may leave the herds seasonally, joining up again at the time of the rut. Within the herds there is a hierarchy between the bulls and dominance is maintained more by threats than actual fighting. Threatening takes the form of holding the head high, nose pointing to the ground, or lateral display of the huge body to the opponent. Head tossing and horn hooking take place and if the opponent does not show submission by lowering its head, fighting may follow. The cows also make these threat displays, but to a lesser extent.

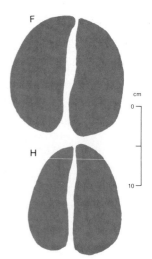

The herds usually move to water in the morning and again in the evening and mud wallowing is often engaged in during the day. Buffalo are predominantly grazers but will take small percentages of browse as well. They are partial to fresh sprouting grass after burns, but will take old grass. They are sensitive to heat and it has been shown that when temperatures reach 40 °C they will cease feeding and move to shade. A great deal of feeding takes place at night. The single young is born during the summer months after a gestation period of 330–346 days. Calf mortality up to two years of age can be high, but thereafter drops to lower levels. **(S328)**

KUDU
(Koedoe)
Tragelaphus strepsiceros

Plate 52
No. 1

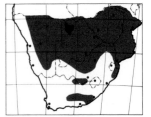

Shoulder height: males 1,4 m, females 1,25 m; mass: males 170–270 kg, females 110–210 kg.

Widespread in the northern, northeastern and parts of the central sector of the Subregion. The kudu is a savanna woodland species and does not occur on open grassland, in forests or desert. It is partial to areas of broken, rocky terrain where there is woodland cover and open water, the latter an essential habitat

---

Plate 52: **1.** Kudu, female and male (p. 190). **2.** Buffalo (p. 189).

1

2

requirement, though it can, however, satisfy its moisture requirements in dry country by eating wild melons and other succulent food.

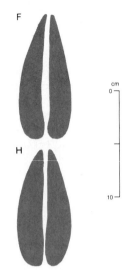

The body colour of the males is fawn grey, the females usually tinged cinnamon, with a series of six to ten unevenly spaced, white transverse stripes on the back and flanks, white facial markings and conspicuous large, broad ears, which are pinkish inside with white fringes. The humped shoulders carry a crest of long hair that continues forward to form a mane on the back of the neck and head, and the males in particular have a fringe of long white-tipped hair on the throat. The tail is pure white underneath, making it very conspicuous in kudu running away from the observer. Only the males have the corkscrew-shaped, spiral horns, which may rise roughly parallel to each other or diverge widely and are such a conspicuous feature of males of this handsome species.

Kudu occur in small herds of up to about 12, four to six being commoner. At the time of the rut the males join the female herds, but at other times are found solitarily or in small bachelor herds of up to about six. They are active in the morning and evening and at night and lie up during the hotter parts of the day. When alarmed they vocalise with a loud harsh bark and the males, when taking to flight, lay their long spiral horns back onto their bodies to avoid contact with low branches. They are accomplished jumpers and can surmount two-metre-high fences with ease.

Kudu are browsers but will eat fresh green grass and are great raiders of grain crops where they can do great damage, trampling as much as they eat. The young may be born at any time throughout the year, although there is a peak during mid-summer. The gestation period is 210 days and the female leaves the herd to give birth in cover. The calves are light cinnamon fawn in colour, with clearly marked white transverse stripes on the back. **(S329)**

SITATUNGA
(Waterkoedoe)
Tragelaphus spekei

Plate 53
No. 2

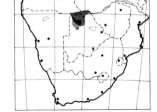

Shoulder height: males 90 cm, females 80 cm; mass: males up to 115 kg, females about 80 kg.

Restricted to the northern parts of the Okavango Swamp in Botswana. The sitatunga is semi-aquatic, spending the greater part of its life in water deep in the swamp.

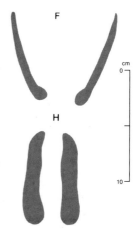

The males are dark brown in colour with a few indistinct lighter coloured blotches of yellowish brown on the back and flanks; the females are either the same colour as the males or redder, with a distinct black band down the mid-back, indistinct transverse white stripes, a white lateral band and white spots on the haunches. The forehead in both sexes is tinged rufous and there are white patches just above the hooves, two on the throat and white facial markings. The hair is long, coarse and shaggy, longest on the neck and the tip of the tail. Only the males have the spiral, keeled horns, which swing back from the head, bow outwards and then swing forward to the yellowish white tips. The keel is well developed and follows the spiral to near the tip.

Owing to the habitat in which sitatunga occur they are difficult to observe. They occur in small loosely knit herds of up to about six, scattering to feed but reforming when disturbed. Active in the cooler parts of the day, at night they may move out of the swamp to feed in the surrounding drier fringes. They rest on matted platforms of broken-down reed stems deep in the reedbeds which they trample down themselves, these often floating in water up to a metre deep. Under stress they are reputed to submerge themselves in water with only their nostrils above the surface and certainly do this when wounded. They are excellent swimmers and take to deep water freely. Their movements through the reedbeds eventually open narrow paths through them.

Sitatunga bark loudly, especially at night; the bark reminiscent of that of bushbuck but more drawn out and repetitive. They are predominantly grazers, feeding on semi-aquatic grasses and the umbels of papyrus and reed shoots, but will take some browse in the form of the fresh leaves of *Acacia* that they find on the swamp fringes and islands. They appear to have their young throughout the year with a peak in mid-winter. The females leave their young on platforms in the swamp or on swamp islands while they feed. **(S330)**

NYALA
Plate 53
(Njala)
No. 1
Tragelaphus angasii

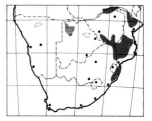

Shoulder height: males 1,1 m, females 1 m; mass: males 90–130 kg, females 55–70 kg.

Occurs only in the northeastern parts of the subregion in dry savanna woodland or where

193

there is a mosaic of open ground, thickets and woodland near floodplains, vleis and rivers.

The males vary in colour from slatey grey to dark brown, with a series of up to 14 white transverse stripes on the back, extending over the flanks, with white spots on the thighs and belly and white markings on the throat and face and upper parts of the limbs. They have long, shaggy, dark brown or black hair on the upper parts of the hind legs, the tail, fringing the under-parts and on the throat, and a mane of long black hair on the upper parts of the neck. The lower part of the legs is yellowish brown, the ears long and tinged reddish on the back. The females are bright chestnut, dark rufous on the top of the muzzle and forehead and with up to 18 white transverse stripes on the body, but

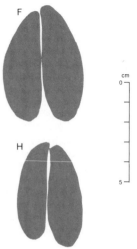

they may or may not have white spots on the thighs and they lack the long hair on the throat and underparts. Only the males have the keeled horns, which spiral upwards from the head, bow outwards, and are smooth towards the white pointed tips.

Nyala occur in groups of 2 or 3, which aggregate to form transient herds of up to 30. Herds of females and juveniles are the most stable but at times break down into family groups. The males are not territorial and the bachelor herds are only short-term associations. The larger aggregations of up to 30 occur in more open country and are usually centred on a preferred feeding area. The males threaten other males by raising the dorsal crest of long hair and spar-ring may take place in the presence of females in oestrus. Their alarm call is a deep bark and they may bleat under stress.

Nyala are predominantly browsers but they will eat grass when it is fresh and green. The males exhibit Flehmen, testing the female's urine for oestrus and in courting will push their heads between the female's back legs, often lifting her hindquarters off the ground. Most matings are by dominant males. The young may be born at any time of the year, with a peak in early and late summer; the gestation period is 220 days. A single calf is born in the cover of thickets. **(S331)**

Plate 53: **1.** Nyala, female and male (p. 193). **2.** Sitatunga (p. 192).

194

53

1

2

BUSHBUCK

(Bosbok)

Tragelaphus scriptus

Plate 54

No. 2

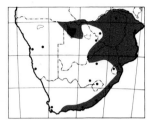

Shoulder height: males 80 cm, females 70 cm; mass: males 40–50 kg, females 25–35 kg.

Occurs in the northern, eastern and southern coastal areas of the Subregion. It has specialised habitat requirements, being associated with riverine and other thickets in the vicinity of water.

Colour and markings vary throughout the range. In the Cape Province the males are dark brown with a few white spots on the flanks and thighs, a crest of yellowish white hair down the mid-back, white facial markings, a white patch on the throat and white under the tail. The females are lighter in colour than the males, the facial markings less distinct. In the northern parts of the subregion the males are much more brightly coloured and are dark red with a profuse pattern of white spots on the shoulders, flanks and thighs and up to eight distinct white transverse lines on the back, the other white markings more distinct than those of males from the Cape Province. The females are rich red with white lines and spots like the males. Throughout their range the old males tend to lose the hair on the sides of the neck, the skin showing through as a dark grey yoke. Only the males have the strongly keeled horns, which are triangular in section and spiral straight upwards.

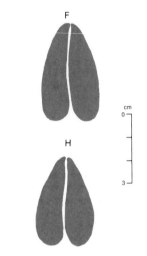

Bushbuck are shy and retiring and commonly occur solitarily or in small groups of two or three. During the heat of the day they lie up in cover, but in overcast weather may be active throughout the day. They have acute senses of sight and smell and persist in close association with human development. Both sexes have a loud, hoarse warning bark. They are predominantly browsers, but will graze on fresh green grass. The young may be born at any time throughout the year, but there is evidence of two peaks of rutting in northern Botswana, with two peaks of births in early and late summer. A single young is born after a gestation period of 180 days and is hidden in thick underbrush where the female suckles it. **(S332)**

Plate 54: **1.** Eland (p. 198). **2.** Bushbuck (p. 196).

54

1

2

ELAND

(Eland)
Taurotragus oryx

Plate 54
No. 1

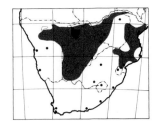

The largest of the African antelope; shoulder height: males 1,7 m, females 1,5 m; mass: males up to 840 kg, females up to 500 kg.

Distribution is restricted to the northern, central and northeastern parts of the Subregion, but the eland is catholic in its habitat requirements and occurs in semi-desert areas as well as in the better-watered eastern parts of the Subregion, on montane situations and in various types of woodland. It avoids forests and, except in transit, open grassland. Water is not an essential requirement as it can obtain its requirements from its food.

Eland are dull fawn coloured and while those from further north in Africa have numerous narrow white transverse stripes on the back, those in the Subregion may have up to five or they may be almost entirely lacking. There is a brown patch on the back of the forelegs, just above the knee, and a patch of long, curly dark brown hair on the forehead, which overlies a glandular area in the skin. There is a band of dark brown along

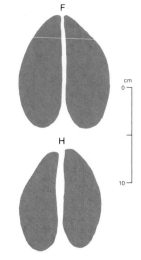

the back, and a tuft of long, similarly coloured hair on the tip of the tail and fringing the dewlap. Both sexes have straight, slightly diverging horns lying in the line of the face, those of the male thick and heavy with a heavy spiral ridge towards the base, those of the female much lighter and tending to be uneven, often slightly curved or splayed outwards.

Eland occur in small herds, which at times join to form huge aggregations that tend to be nomadic. Their social organisation has not been studied in depth, but indications from introduced populations show that during the summer the nursery herds of females and juveniles are joined by several males from the bachelor herds to form breeding herds. After calving the bulls leave the breeding herd to return to the bachelor herds. Dominance in both sexes is displayed by ritual behaviour such as shaking of the head, slapping with the horns or charging with lowered horns. Fighting between adult males can lead to fatal injuries. They are prodigious jumpers and when the adult males walk, a characteristic clicking noise can be heard, the origin of which has been the subject of some controversy. It appears to come from the knees.

Eland are predominantly browsers, but are partial to fresh sprouting grass. The young may be born at any time of the year, with a peak that varies with locality during the early summer months. The gestation period is about 271 days. Twins are rare, and although females are often closely accompanied by several young they will only suckle their own calves. The young have longer hair than the adults, tending to be reddish fawn. **(S333)**

Subfamily **REDUNCINAE**. There are five members of this Subfamily; one large, the waterbuck, and four medium-sized, the reedbuck, mountain reedbuck, red lechwe and puku. They are all associated with open water and are confined in their distribution to Africa south of the Sahara. Only the males have horns, which lack keels or spiralling and are either bowed, lyrate or hooked. Pre-orbital glands are absent, except in the puku, where they are poorly developed, and pedal glands are either absent or rudimentary. The females have two pairs of mammae.

REEDBUCK　　　　　　Plate 55
(Rietbok)　　　　　　　　No. 2
Redunca arundinum

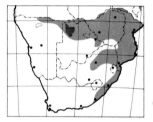

F

Shoulder height: males 90 cm, females 80 cm; mass: males 40–70 kg, females 30–50 kg.

Occurs in the northern and eastern parts of the Subregion. It has specialised habitat requirements and occurs only where there is open water with cover in the form of stands of tall grass or reed beds. As a consequence, its occurrence is patchy and discontinuous.

The colour of the upper parts varies from greyish brown to buffy yellow, the back often slightly darker than the remainder of the body. The underparts, chin and facial markings are white, the upper parts of the throat with a light coloured crescent-shaped marking, which is more distinct in the males. The front of the fore and the lower part of the hind legs is dark brown. The tail is characteristically bushy and is buffy yellow above and white below. Only the males have horns, which curve evenly forward, tending to be hooked forward at the tips, and are ridged and corrugated for their basal two thirds. In some populations there is a distinct bare glandular patch below the ears.

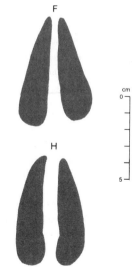

H

cm
0

5

199

Reedbuck live in pairs or family parties, although during the cold, dry months of May to August temporary associations of several family parties may take place. A pair occupy a territory, from which the male will actively chase off other males, mostly by threat displays. These may take the form of displaying the white band on the throat, while standing facing or sideways to the trespasser, or of using this display while urinating or defecating, which is considered by authorities to be one of the strongest threats. The male may also whistle and stott or may threaten with his horns. This may lead to fighting, which never, however, seems to become serious.

During the dry season reedbuck are more active during the day than during the summer months, when they are predominantly nocturnal. They whistle loudly, the females sometimes clicking and whistling. During the heat of the day they lie up either in the open or in the shelter of tall grass. They are predominantly grazers, but will browse when grass is in short supply. The young may be born at any time of the year, with peaks depending on the locality. A single lamb is born after a gestation period of about seven and a half months; it hides itself in tall grass and is visited by the female for suckling once a day. **(S334)**

MOUNTAIN REEDBUCK
(Rooiribbok)
Redunca fulvorufula

Plate 55
No. 1

Shoulder height: males 75 cm, females 70 cm; mass: males 24–37 kg, females 15–34 kg.

Occurs in the southeastern and eastern parts of the Subregion, with a small relict population in southeastern Botswana. It lives on the grass-covered, stony slopes of hills and mountains where there is some cover in the form of trees or bushes, the availability of water being an essential habitat requirement.

The upper parts of the body are greyish, the underparts white, the head and neck yellower than the remainder of the body. The coat is soft and woolly, the bushy tail greyish above and white below, and there are bare glandular patches on the sides of the head below the base of the ears. Only the males have the short, heavily ridged horns, which hook forward at about the level of the top of the ears.

Mountain reedbuck occur in herds of up to 30

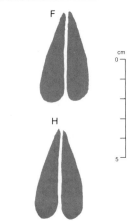

Plate 55: **1.** Mountain reedbuck (p. 200). **2.** Reedbuck (p. 199).

but more usually in groups of 3 to 6 together. They are grazers with seasonal preferences for various types of grasses. Active about sunrise and sunset, they rest up during the day in the shelter of bushes, in tight groups. Their social organisation consists of territorial and non-territorial males, nursery herds of females and juveniles, and bachelor herds. The territorial males occupy territories of up to 28 ha on a year-round basis, only leaving them to feed in adjacent areas or when moved by fire. Non-territorial males may remain solitary or join up with the bachelor herds. The nursery herds may move over the territories of several males, who try to retain females by herding them. The territorial male courts the female with his head outstretched towards her and she may submit by lowering her head if she is receptive. The young may be born at any time of the year after a gestation period of 236–251 days. The female leaves the herd to give birth to the single young, which hides itself in thick cover. **(S335)**

WATERBUCK

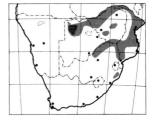

Plate 56
No. 3

(Waterbok, Kringgat)
Kobus ellipsiprymnus

The largest member of this Subfamily; shoulder height: males 1,3 m; mass: males 250–270 kg, the females slightly smaller and lighter.

The waterbuck has a limited distribution in the northern and northeastern parts of the Sub-region, on floodplains, vleis and grassy areas along rivers, seldom more than 2 km from open water.

Greyish brown in colour with white throat and facial markings; the characteristic feature is the broad white ring encircling the rump. Only the males have horns, which sweep forward from the head in an even curve and are heavily ridged but smooth towards the tips.

Waterbuck occur in small herds of up to about 12, occasionally up to 30. Their social organisation consists of territorial males, nursery herds of females and juveniles and bachelor herds of non-territorial and juvenile males and occasionally juvenile females. The territorial males hold territories, which vary in diameter from 1,2 to 2,8 km, throughout the year, deterring the entry

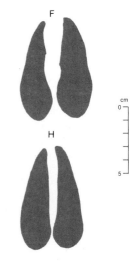

of other adult males by intimidatory displays or occasionally by fighting. The nursery herds may wander over the territories of several territorial males, which attempt to hold them by herding. The bachelor herds move widely and are generally tolerated by the territorial males. The herds tend to fragment during the winter months when food is scarce.

Waterbuck are predominantly grazers but their diet includes a proportion of browse. The territorial males exhibit Flehmen, courting the females in oestrus by face and horn rubbing. They breed throughout the year, a single young or occasionally twins being born after a gestation period of 280 days. The female leaves the herd to give birth in seclusion. The juveniles are reddish in colour.

(S336)

RED LECHWE
(Rooi-lechwe)
Kobus leche

Plate 56
No. 2

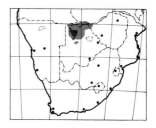

Shoulder height 1 m, mean mass: males 118 kg, females 74 kg.

Occurs in the vicinity of the Okavango Swamp and the swamps associated with the Chobe River in northern Botswana. It is a water-loving species, spending a large part of its life in the shallower water of the swamps or in their immediate vicinity.

The upper parts of the body are reddish yellow in colour, the underparts pure white, and there are dark markings on the front of the forelegs and a black tuft of hair on the end of the tail. The throat, chin and facial markings are white. Only the males have the lyrate horns, which are heavily ridged, with smooth tips. The hooves are elongated, although not to the extent seen in the sitatunga, an adaptation to walking on muddy substrate.

Red lechwe occur in herds of up to about 20, these aggregating to form huge concentrations numbering in the hundreds. The herds are loose associations and tend to break up and reform. The social organisation consists of territorial males, nursery and bachelor herds. At the time

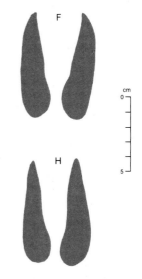

of the rut the territorial male defends a territory with a diameter of up to about 100 m for a limited period, mainly by threatening trespassing males by intimidatory displays but sometimes by serious fighting which may lead to the death of combatants. The nursery herds, consisting of females and juveniles, may move over several of these territories unless herded by the male. The bachelor herds consist of non-territorial males, juvenile males and occasionally females. A territorial male may allow other adult males to enter his territory providing they do not show interest in his females.

Active around sunrise and sunset, red lechwe usually rest on dry ground during the heat of the day. They take to the shelter of the swamp if disturbed. When in motion the males have the characteristic habit of laying their horns back on the shoulders, the muzzle pointed forward, which no doubt helps them move through reed beds. Red lechwe are grazers living on swamp grasses. They breed throughout the year with a peak, in Botswana, during the early summer months when the single young is born in the cover of tall grass on swamp islands. Gestation is 225 days. **(S337)**

PUKU
(Poekoe)
Kobus vardonii

Plate 56
No. 1

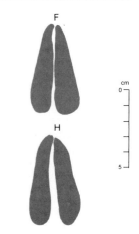

Shoulder height: males 92 cm, females 84 cm; mass: males 65–78 kg, females 50–78 kg.

Confined to a small area on the south bank of the Chobe River in northeastern Botswana, the Pookoo Flats, on dry grassy floodplain in the immediate vicinity of open water.

The upper parts of the body are golden yellow, the underparts pure white, the throat, muzzle and facial markings white, the forehead tinged brown. It lacks the dark bands down the forelegs seen in the red lechwe and is more brightly coloured. Only the males have the lyrate horns, which are heavier and shorter than those of the red lechwe, but similarly heavily ridged, with smooth tips. There are preorbital glands in front of the eyes and well-developed, deep inguinal glands.

Puku occur in small herds numbering up to about six, which are unstable as individuals may leave and later rejoin either the same herd or another. The territorial males may defend territories from a few days up to several months, but not always continuously. While they may allow other

---

Plate 56: **1.** Puku (p. 204). **2.** Red lechwe (p. 203). **3.** Waterbuck (p. 202).

males to trespass they more usually chase them away by demonstrations including tail wagging and horn slashing. The nursery herds consist of adult and juvenile females and may move over the territories of several males. The bachelor herds, which consist of non-territorial and juvenile males, keep clear of the territories of the territorial males and the ranges of the nursery herds. Females in oestrus are courted by the male, who approaches her with his horns laid back and inserts his front leg between her back legs to tap her abdomen.

Puku are active around sunrise and sunset, resting up during the hottest time of the day in the open. Unlike waterbuck and red lechwe, puku will associate with other bovids, especially impala. They are grazers. The young may be born at any time throughout the year, after a gestation period of about 240 days, and are left in concealment while the female feeds. The females make little effort to defend newborn calves. **(S338)**

REFERENCE SECTION

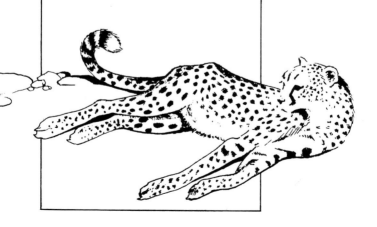

GLOSSARY

adpressed	lying closely applied to a surface.
ambient	surrounding.
anterior	to the front.
antitragus	a lobe of skin near the base of the outer fringe of the ear in bats.
arboreal	living in or adapted to living in trees.
biotic zone	a continuous geographic area that contains ecological associations distinguishable from those of adjacent zones, especially at the species and subspecies level.
bulla	a globular, capsular bone housing the structures of the middle and inner ear, situated on the underside of the skull.
callosity	a hardened, thickened area of skin.
cheekteeth	those teeth lying behind the canine teeth.
commensal	an organism living with another and sharing the same food, one or both benefiting by the association.
digit	a finger or toe in mammals.
dorsal	on or pertaining to the back.
feral	wild, escaped from domestication or introduced and reverted to the wild state.
Flehmen	an act performed by some mammals in which the upper lip is retracted, the nostrils wrinkled, the head perhaps raised and the tongue sometimes moved rhythmically. This opens ducts leading to the Jacobsen's organ and pumps chemicals into it for sensory detection. Flehmen is often used by adult males to test a female's reproductive condition by detecting chemicals from her vulva or urine.
foxing	a fading of the colour of hair, which imparts a reddish tinge to it.
gregarious	living together in colonies or other types of assemblages.
habitat	the kind of place, with respect to vegetation and climate, in which a given species lives.
home range	the area over which an animal travels in pursuit of its routine activities.
inguinal glands	glands situated in the groin, i.e. the area between the lower lateral part of the abdomen and the thigh.
interfemoral	situated between the legs. Applies in particular to the membrane between the hind legs of bats.

Jacobsen's organ	chemical sense organ lying between the mouth and nasal passages and connected to one or both of them. Brought into use by Flehmen.
mammae	strictly the milk-bearing glands, but usually represented by the nipples alone.
mandible	the lower jaw.
metatarsal glands	glands situated on the hind legs of mammals on the ankle joint.
murids (Muridae)	a Family of rodents that, with the Family Cricetidae, includes the rats and mice.
muzzle	the part of the face that lies in front of the eyes.
nipple clinging	the act of some young murids, which remain in a state of semi-permanent attachment to the nipples of the female after birth.
nuchal patch	a patch of hair on the nape of hares and some rabbits, which contrasts in colour with that of the upper parts of the body.
oestrus	period during which a female mammal is sexually receptive and mating will usually lead to conception.
pedal glands	glands situated in the feet, between the cloven hooves.
pelage	the hairy coat.
pinna	the external ear flap or conch.
posterior	to the back, behind.
preorbital	anterior to the eye socket.
preorbital glands	glands situated just in front of the eyes.
prehensile	capable of grasping.
preputial glands	glands situated adjacent to the penis or vaginal opening.
proximal	closer to a given point.
rhinarium	the naked fleshy area on the tip of the muzzle that encloses the nostrils.
rostrum	that portion of the skull which lies anterior to the eye sockets, the upper portion of the muzzle.
species	composed of potentially or actually interbreeding populations of animals.
thermoregulation	a mammal's ability to regulate its body temperature under differing ambient temperatures.
tragus	a small cartilaginous process found in the external opening of the ear in bats.

USEFUL REFERENCES

Apps, P.J. In press. *Wild Ways: A Fieldguide to Mammal Behaviour in Southern Africa.* Halfway House: Southern Book Publishers.

Dorst, J. and Dandelot, P. 1970. *A Fieldguide to the Larger Mammals of Africa.* London: Collins.

Grobler, H., Hall-Martin, A. and Walker, C. 1984. *Predators of Southern Africa.* Johannesburg: Macmillan.

Haltenorth, T. and Diller, H. 1980. *A Field Guide to the Mammals of Africa including Madagascar.* London: Collins.

Lynch, C.D. 1983. "The mammals of the Orange Free State". *Memoirs of the National Museum, Bloemfontein, No. 18.*

Meester, J.A.J., Rautenbach, I.L., Dippenaar, N.J. and Baker, C. 1986. "Classification of southern African mammals". *Transvaal Museum Monograph 5: 1–359.*

Meester, J.A.J. and Setzer, H.W. 1971. *The Mammals of Africa: An Identification Manual.* City of Washington, D.C.: Smithsonian Institution Press.

Pienaar, U. de V., Rautenbach, I.L. and de Graaff, G. 1980. *The Small Mammals of the Kruger National Park.* Pretoria: National Parks Board of South Africa.

Rautenbach, I.L. 1983. *Mammals of the Transvaal.* Pretoria: Ecoplan.

Roberts, A. 1951. *The Mammals of South Africa.* Cape Town: Central News Agency.

Rowe-Rowe, D.T. 1981. "The small carnivores of Natal". *Lammergeyer* 25: 1–48.

Smithers, R.H.N. 1966. *The Mammals of Rhodesia, Zambia and Malawi.* London: Collins.

Smithers, R.H.N. 1971: "The mammals of Botswana". *Museum Memoir No. 4, National Museums of Rhodesia.*

Smithers, R.H.N. 1983. *The Mammals of the Southern African Subregion.* Pretoria: The University of Pretoria.

Smithers, R.H.N. and Tello, José L.P.L. 1976. "Check list and atlas of the mammals of Mocambique". *Museum Memoir No. 8, National Museums and Monuments of Rhodesia.*

Smithers, R.H.N. and Wilson, V.J., 1979. "Check list and atlas of the mammals of Zimbabwe/Rhodesia". *Museum Memoir No. 9, National Museums and Monuments of Rhodesia.*

Stuart, C.T. 1981. "Notes on the mammalian carnivores of the Cape Province, South Africa". *Bontebok* 1: 1–58.

Walker, C. 1981. *Signs of the Wild: Field Guide to the Tracks and Signs of Mammals of Southern Africa.* Johannesburg: Natural History Publications.

INDEX OF SCIENTIFIC NAMES

INDEX OF ENGLISH NAMES

INDEX OF AFRIKAANS NAMES